GOD'S CONSTANT PRESENCE

True Stories of Everyday Miracles

———— ♦ ————

Wrapped
in His Protection

GOD'S CONSTANT PRESENCE

True Stories of Everyday Miracles

Wrapped in His Protection

EDITORS OF GUIDEPOSTS

Guideposts

A Gift from Guideposts

Thank you for your purchase! We appreciate your support and want to express our gratitude with a special gift just for you.

Dive into *Spirit Lifters*, a complimentary booklet that will fortify your faith and offer solace during challenging moments. It contains 31 carefully selected verses from scripture that will soothe your soul and uplift your spirit.

Please use the QR code or go to **guideposts.org/spiritlifters** to download.

Wrapped in His Protection

Published by Guideposts
100 Reserve Road, Suite E200
Danbury, CT 06810
Guideposts.org

Copyright © 2025 by Guideposts. All rights reserved.

This book, or parts thereof, may not be reproduced, stored in a retrieval system, or transmitted in any form or by any means, electronic, mechanical, photocopying, recording or otherwise, without the written permission of the publisher.

Cover design by Serena Fox Design Company
Interior design by Serena Fox Design Company
Cover photo debibishop / Getty Images
Typeset by Aptara, Inc.

ISBN 978-1-961442-18-4 (hardcover)
ISBN 978-1-961442-19-1 (softcover)
ISBN 978-1-961442-20-7 (epub)

Printed and bound in the United States of America
$PrintCode

I will say of the Lord, "He is my refuge and my fortress, my God, in whom I trust." Surely he will save you from the fowler's snare and from the deadly pestilence. He will cover you with his feathers, and under his wings you will find refuge; his faithfulness will be your shield and rampart.

—*Psalm 91:2-4 (NIV)*

TABLE *of* CONTENTS

Introduction 1
    Out of the Fire

Chapter 1. 11
    Protected by His Hand

Chapter 2. 45
    God Travels with You

Chapter 3. 103
    God Sends His Helpers

Chapter 4. 151
    Sustained and Healed

Chapter 5. 205
    Guided to Safety

Contributors 243

Acknowledgments 245

Out of the Fire
Jeannie Blackmer

DECEMBER 30, 2021, is a day I will never forget. I had begun my post-Christmas clean-up by taking our Christmas decorations down and placing them in plastic bins for storage. The ornaments from our Christmas tree would be sorted into different plastic ornament bins, one for each of our adult sons and one for my husband, Zane, and me. One of my sons, who was married, had asked to have his own set of ornaments for next year. I decided it would be a good time to create a set for each of them and just keep ours with us. I loved our family ornaments and especially treasured some I had from my childhood that my mother had hand-painted.

Zane and I also had post-Christmas Covid. Zane was feeling worse than I was, so we had hired Rocky Mountain Medics, a mobile IV therapy service, to come to our home and give him a vitamin infusion in hopes of boosting his immunity and speeding up his recovery. When the two medics arrived, they mentioned they had seen some power lines arcing at an intersection a mile from our home, probably due to the gale-force winds we were experiencing. We weren't that concerned because Boulder, Colorado, is known to have strong winds. We'd seen arcing before, but, still, our antennae were up and we knew to keep an eye on that.

As the medics gave Zane his infusion, I continued my project in the basement, occasionally distracted by the violent winds rattling our windows. The doorbell rang. *I wonder who that is?* We weren't expecting any visitors.

I went upstairs and opened the front door, but no one was there. I noticed the smell of smoke in the air. Alarmed, I went to find the medics. "Did one of you ring the doorbell just now?"

"Yes," one of them replied. "I went out to get something from our van, and the door locked behind me."

"Did the air smell smoky to you?"

"Yes, it did."

I decided to go out and take a look for the source of the smell. Due to the powerful winds, I could barely step forward, but I made it to a point past our detached garage where I looked down on the hillside below. Our house sat on 11 acres on the top of a mesa surrounded by open space. I could see thick dark smoke heading up the hillside toward us.

I hurried back inside. "You better hurry up this infusion," I told the medics. "I think there's a fire."

Worried, Zane called 911 and the operator said, "Get out now!"

At this point, everything happened fast. The men finished Zane's infusion using a thicker tube for the IV as I grabbed a "go box" that held our passports, marriage certificate, social security cards, immunization records, car titles, and other important papers, and sat it by the front door. As the medics left, they asked if we needed help, and I said "No, just go!" Later, I regretted not asking them to grab a few things.

Zane had put our chocolate Labrador, Ody, on a leash and taken him and our go-box to the car. As he went out,

I remembered some advice from a friend who lived in the mountains and had recently evacuated due to a wildfire. She mentioned she had grabbed her laundry basket because it had her family's most recently worn clothes and everything they would need for a day or two. Zane came back in and I told him my plan to go downstairs and get our laundry.

"No," he told me firmly. "The wind is blowing 100 miles per hour and the fire will be here any minute. We have to go NOW!"

The fear on Zane's face and urgency of his words awakened me to our reality. I hustled to the car as ash fell on me. The dark smoke I saw below now enveloped our home. The gusts of wind and the acrid smoke smell made it hard to breathe. Once in the car with Ody, I looked over my shoulder and watched Zane run to us carrying his favorite guitar, ash blowing and raining down on him.

We started down our driveway, which is about a half-mile long and runs down a hill with natural grasses and pine trees on each side. Smoke cloaked our car, making it as dark as nighttime. We could barely see the road. Once we made it down the driveway, we turned left, because we knew the fire was coming from the right. We made our way to a road below our house that was parallel to where our home sat. Once we were no longer in the dark smoke, I glanced up to our home and saw it engulfed in flames. It had maybe been 7 minutes since we had left. We pulled into a dirt parking lot with tears streaming down our faces and watched our home burn as the fire swept across the grassy hillside, destroying everything in its path.

We decided to go to our son's place, about 20 miles away. Because so many people were evacuating their homes, it took us several hours to get there. We arrived with only the clothes on our backs, our dog, my purse with my phone, our box with important papers, and Zane's guitar. We reeked of smoke, so I went upstairs to shower. When I looked in the mirror, I saw ash in the corners of my eyes.

Later, some friends showed up with a meal and items we would need for the next couple of days, including winter coats, underwear, toiletries, and more. I cried myself to sleep.

The Aftermath

WHEN I AWOKE, I heard that the Marshall Fire, as it had been named, destroyed 1,084 homes. By that evening the fire was finally stopped due to the hard work of the firefighters and a snowstorm. We were thankful to be alive, yet disheartened to have lost everything we owned, especially the irreplaceable sentimental items—the Christmas ornaments I had spent the morning meticulously organizing for future holidays, our old photos taken on film, our boys' memory boxes, our wedding album, and so much more.

Due to the extensive damage throughout our community and the potential remaining hot spots from the fire, it took a few days for the National Guard to allow us to safely return to our property to see the damage. It wasn't only our home I concerned about; because I'm a beekeeper, I was anxious to know if my bees had survived. I doubted it, but wanted to check on them.

After getting the OK to return to our home, we found complete devastation. Our property and home now resembled a war zone. I stood on twisted blackened metal and saw ash blanketing the ground and piles of rubble strewn around the area. I took a deep breath to calm my nerves, but it was cut short as I was overcome with the sickening smell of smoke. Our home was gone. In its place was a giant hole, as if a bomb had dropped in that spot. What hadn't blown around sat in the depths of that hole. We walked our property, searching through the dusty ash for any items that might have survived, but we found nothing of value. A firefighter had told me that forest fires can reach 2,000 degrees Fahrenheit or hotter. The fire had been so hot it melted metal, and even our fire safes couldn't withstand the length and intensity of it. I saw the mangled remains of our bed on top of the ash heap and choked back a sob. If the fire had been during the night, we would have been asleep on that bed. Because we had no warning and our home was engulfed so quickly, I'm not sure we would have escaped. This was the moment where I started to grasp how God had protected us.

My beehives were not far from our house so we went to look. I didn't imagine my bees surviving this intense fire. When I approached the apiary, I saw that the lilac bushes that grew behind the hive boxes and the wooden railroad ties surrounding them had burned. The winds had blown the hives off their stands, but because I used straps to hold the stacked wooden boxes in place, they were still held together. I asked Zane and my son, Josh, to hoist the hives back onto their stands. When they began to lift the first hive, bees flew out! I was ecstatic. My bees had miraculously survived. We were not the only ones God had protected. As I watched my bees fly around and then back into their home, I felt hope. Eventually, we would have a home again.

We continued to search our property, but everywhere we looked, everything was charred. Even the ground where wild grasses grew was blackened. We counted 171 burned trees. I knew at this moment that the recovery from this loss was going to be a marathon, not a sprint.

God Is the Protector

God sweetly spoke to me through His Word, giving me strength and hope as I recovered from the loss and trauma of the fire.

One Bible story that resonated for me in a fresh way was the familiar story of Shadrach, Meshach, and Abednego in Daniel chapter three. These three brave men refused to bow down and worship the golden image that King Nebuchadnezzar created, knowing the consequence of disobedience was being tossed into a fiery furnace. Yet they choose to obey God and not the king. Nebuchadnezzar, filled with fury, ordered the furnace to be heated seven times more than usual. It was so hot that the soldiers who tied them up in their clothes and cast them into the fiery furnace died when they threw them in. Then God did something amazing:

> King Nebuchadnezzar was astonished and rose up in haste. He declared to his counsellors, "Did we not cast three men bound into the fire?" They answered and said to the king, "True, O king." He answered and said, "But I see four men unbound, walking in the midst of the fire, and they are not hurt; and the appearance of the fourth is like a son of the gods."
>
> Then Nebuchadnezzar came near to the door of the burning fiery furnace; he declared, "Shadrach, Meshach, and Abednego, servants of the Most High God, come out, and come here!" Then Shadrach, Meshach, and Abednego came out from the fire. And the satraps, the prefects, the governors, and the king's counsellors gathered together and saw that the fire had not had any power over the bodies of those men. The hair of their heads was not singed, their cloaks

were not harmed, and no smell of fire had come upon them. (Daniel 3:24–27, ESV)

This story assured me of how powerful our God is. Nothing limits His sovereignty. When Shadrach, Meshach, and Abednego came out of the furnace, they had no singed hair, none of their clothes were damaged, and they didn't even smell of smoke. In the same way, even though all of our belongings were destroyed, and everything on us and with us—our clothes, hair, car, dog, everything—smelled of smoke, we survived. After experiencing a destructive fire firsthand, I now have a better understanding of what a miracle God did for Shadrach, Meshach, and Abednego. Not only did he save them from a tremendously hot fire, but no evidence of being in a fire remained upon them. Nothing limits the power of God.

And these men were not alone in the fire. Nebuchadnezzar saw four men unbound and walking through the flames. The fourth looked like a "son of the gods." Jesus was with them in the fire as He is with us. He is truly Immanuel, God with us.

Even in the chaos of evacuating, I'm confident God was with us. The two men who came to give Zane his infusion saw arcing on the road below, giving us a warning we otherwise wouldn't have had. I heard a doorbell ring, and that prompted me to go outside and notice the approaching smoke. I didn't go downstairs to get our laundry. The fire occurred during the day rather than at night, when we would have been asleep. The fire hadn't spread so quickly that it blocked our driveway, and because we were forewarned we knew which way to turn to drive away from it. Counting all of our blessings gave me an unexplainable sense of peace.

During the journey of recovery while we rebuilt our destroyed home, God used His Word to speak specifically to me and my unique experience, filling me with strength and hope. So many scriptures took on new meaning and encouraged me:

> When you pass through the waters, I will be with you; and through the rivers, they shall not overwhelm you; when you walk through fire you shall not be burned, and the flame shall not consume you. (Isaiah 43:2, ESV)

> ... to grant to those who mourn in Zion—to give them a beautiful headdress instead of ashes, the oil of gladness instead of mourning, the garment of praise instead of a faint spirit. (Isaiah 61:3, ESV)

> For we know that if the earthly tent we live in is destroyed, we have a building from God, an eternal house in heaven, not built by human hands. (2 Corinthians 5:1, NIV)

> And the LORD will guide you continually and satisfy your desire in scorched places. (Isaiah 58:11, ESV)

> "One's life does not consist in the abundance of his possessions." (Luke 12:15, ESV)

In the midst of having so much taken away from me in this fire, I have felt closer to God than ever. After experiencing His protection, I've also experienced His goodness. I have a relationship with a personal, loving God who gives me hope and never leaves me.

Our new home will be built on a strong foundation, but spiritually our foundation is God, and our life will be built on Him. We'll rebuild and replace much of what we lost, such as our Christmas ornaments. They won't be exactly what we had, but that seems less important now. We are thankful we survived. And because God is good, He is with us always and everywhere. I believe this, and I pray you do too.

May the perfect grace and eternal love of Christ our Lord be our never-failing protection and help.

—Saint Ignatius

CHAPTER 1

Protected by His Hand

Refuge on the Highway 12
   Jessica Andrus Lindstrom

Halo of Protection 18
   Heidi Chiavaroli

My Baby's Shield 22
   Kristen Paris

Man's Bullets vs. God's Armor 26
   Joe Fletcher

The Day God Saved My Life 31
   Robin Ayscue

Always by Our Side 35
   Linda Marie

The Man with Nine Lives 40
   John Peterson, as told to Wendy Lynn Smith

Refuge on the Highway
Jessica Andrus Lindstrom

The smell of apple blossoms hung in the air on the warm morning when my husband, Tim, and I packed the car, strapped our one-year-old son, Carl, into his cushioned car seat, and hugged Tim's parents goodbye. A long drive awaited us as we departed his family's farm in Michigan back to our home in Virginia. I climbed into the passenger side and buckled my seatbelt, careful not to disturb Franny, the motley-colored cat curled up at my feet.

Tim beeped the horn as he headed down the driveway past the large weeping willow in front of the yellow, clapboard farmhouse. I rolled down my window, waving a white tissue with my outstretched fingers until my in-laws were out of sight.

"Bye-Bye!" sang our son as I retracted my arm and closed the window. "Bye-Bye!"

I dabbed my eyes with the tissue. Leaving the farm and Tim's parents was always bittersweet. Yes, I was eager to get back to our farm and all that awaited us there but reluctant to leave behind the elderly couple who were facing recent health challenges and knew, as we did, that they would not live long enough to see their only grandchild grown. Tim's mother was almost 90—23 years older than my parents. Would we see them again? I prayed fervently that we would but acknowledged in silence, still dabbing my eyes, that I couldn't know the day or hour when any of our times on this earth would end.

Our Easter week at the farm had passed quickly. We had picked daffodils, walked the tree-lined lane nestled between fields sown with soybeans and corn, and celebrated the season with an egg hunt on Easter morning followed by a delicious ham dinner prepared by Tim's father. Packed with the luggage in the back of the station wagon was a plump yellow chicken—a stuffed animal larger than our son—that his grandparents had given him on Easter morning. It chirped when hugged and, it seemed, when jostled by bumps in the road as we sped along.

"Chickie! Chickie!" Carl crooned delightedly, reaching toward the sound and clapping his hands.

Before long he had fallen asleep, his soft breathing mingled with the snores coming from Franny, who still slumbered at my feet, and from the periodic chirping of the chicken.

> **The LORD will keep you from all harm—he will watch over your life; the LORD will watch over your coming and going both now and forevermore.**
>
> —PSALM 121:7–8 (NIV)

My husband and I talked about the week and our desire to persuade his parents to move in with us, a subject we had not yet broached with them but were feeling compelled to suggest. We fell silent, lost in our own thoughts, staring ahead at the divider lines on the black pavement slipping swiftly and hypnotically under the car. I sighed, pulled out a book and began to read while we drove steadily eastward and then southward, eventually entering Ohio.

After stopping at a rest area where we changed and fed Carl, Tim asked me to drive for a spell so he could nap. We swapped places, and after settling into the driver's side I was joined by Franny, who curled up on my lap under the steering wheel and promptly fell back asleep. It wasn't long before Tim and Carl were dozing, too.

As I pulled out onto I-70, I was still thinking about Tim's parents, seeing in my mind the two of them standing in the driveway waving to us as we left—two figures becoming smaller and smaller in the sideview mirror until they disappeared completely. Was that image a sign? Did it mean this really was the last time we would see them together? I tried to push such thoughts from my mind. It was pointless to envision a future I had no knowledge of or control over. I took a deep breath and thanked God for the time we had just spent with them and for whatever time we still had left together.

> God is our refuge and strength, an ever-present help in trouble.
>
> —PSALM 46:1 (NIV)

Traffic had increased measurably since our early morning start. Long lines of semitrailers dominated the right-hand lanes of the four-lane highway. The sight was mesmerizing, like trains of containers zipping by at a railroad crossing. I joined the cars in the far left-hand lane to avoid the trucks and slower moving vehicles to the right, settling into a speed of 75 mph, keeping pace with the cars I was following.

The sun streaming through the side windows was bright; the inside of the car, toasty warm. Dropping one hand from the steering wheel, I stroked the sleeping cat in my lap without taking my eyes off the road and started humming to myself. A peaceful calm enveloped me.

It was the vibrations of the rumble strips on the far lefthand side of the road that jolted me awake. At first, I had no idea where I was, and then I knew—the car was drifting off the road. My hands clutched the steering wheel as I started to brake and swerve to the right, trying to get back into my lane. I could hear a distant voice—my husband's?—telling me not to slam my foot on the brakes but to pump them lightly and not to turn the steering wheel if I could help it. But I couldn't help it. I couldn't control anything. I clung to the wheel and prayed.

> **Keep me safe, my God, for in you I take refuge.**
>
> —PSALM 16:1 (NIV)

The car veered to the right in what seemed like slow motion. I saw sky and pavement, my whitened knuckles on the wheel, and the dashboard with its illuminated dials. The car continued to turn in a slow arc across the four lanes of traffic. I closed my eyes as we spun and continued to pray.

Then, suddenly, we came to a stop. I opened my eyes. We were facing forward, astonishingly sandwiched neatly into a gap in the guardrails on the other side of the interstate. It was as if the car had been caught up by larger-than-life hands and gently placed in safety on the grassy shoulder. My husband and I sat in stupefied silence. Our son slept on.

GOD'S GIFT OF SIGHT
— Eryn Lynum —

ARTISTS ARE OFTEN known for their signature style. Van Gogh, for example, was famed for big, bold brush strokes, particularly in swirls across night skies. Leonardo da Vinci was famed for his expressive, realistic representation of his subjects; Jackson Pollock, on the other end of the spectrum, used wholly abstract forms that could look like paint splatters.

One can also glimpse God's signature styles in His creations—the way that the building blocks of His world show up again and again. For example, lemongrass is named for its trademark citric aroma, but it is unrelated to lemon trees. Lemongrass and lemon trees, along with lemon verbena and lemon tea-tree, have a compound called citral that gives them their familiar and pleasant lemon aroma. Unrelated plant species carrying similar characteristics and compounds are beautiful examples of God's signature marks across creation, the little signs of His work that we can see in our everyday lives.

Then the sound of engines pierced the stillness as a stream of semitrailers at breakneck speed roared past on our left, their drivers apparently unaware that a car had just circled in front of them. I shook my head in disbelief. My last memory before falling asleep was of a highway filled with traffic. How was it possible that when I dozed and lost control the lanes were empty, allowing us to circle unscathed and land lightly and miraculously into a break in the guardrails? We could so easily have hit one side or the other had we landed but a foot or two closer to either one.

Without prompting, my husband and I instinctively reached for the other's hands and bowed our heads. Aloud my husband spoke what my mind had been repeating like a mantra since the car had stopped.

"Thank You, God, for protecting us in this time of peril."

"Yes, thank You," I echoed softly and then added, lifting my head: "This could so easily have been the end of our lives, but God saved us for a purpose. Let's visit your parents again as soon as possible so we can talk with them about moving in with us."

Tim nodded and squeezed my hands. We exited the car cautiously to change places, still bewildered by our narrow escape.

As I slipped back into the passenger seat, I winced, feeling for the first time a dull, smarting sensation on my legs. Upon closer examination, I discovered multiple punctures in both of my upper thighs, some still moist with blood. When the rumble strips had awakened me, they had also startled Franny. As the car spun, she had kept her balance by literally clinging for dear life to my thighs with her claws. I hadn't felt a thing.

Suddenly, I began to cry, overwhelmed by the experience and the realization that this was hardly a close call, but proof instead of God's constant presence in my life.

I had more living in God's name to do.

Halo of Protection
Heidi Chiavaroli

Planting my feet firmly on the gym floor, I bent my knees slightly and positioned my hands in front of me in anticipation of the volleyball that might come my way. I inhaled a deep breath and glanced at my high-school peers—girls in gym shorts and T-shirts—*healthy* girls, girls I'd felt quite separated from the last few months.

I swallowed and tried to focus on the ball coming over the net, saying a small prayer that it would *not* come to me. Over the last several weeks, I'd gotten more adept at volleying prayers than balls. A grand mal seizure had caused me to miss 4 days of school, but it was the subsequent headaches I endured from a spinal tap done in the hospital that had completely tripped me up and set me back. For weeks, I suffered unbearable pain whenever upright. Unable to sit in classes or stand without the headaches attacking me, I fell hopelessly behind. Colleges placed a lot of emphasis on junior-year grades. What would happen if I didn't make the cut? The stress only created fertile ground for more seizures.

As we worked with my neurologist to get my medication levels right so that the seizures would be under control, and as I underwent a second spinal procedure to alleviate the headaches, I formed a habit of prayer. In my weakness and inadequacy, I turned to God. This was new for me—depending on Him so needfully, listening intently for His voice, His assurance.

All my life, I had been capable and self-reliant. If I wanted good grades, I'd study harder. If I wanted to improve my cross-country times, I'd put in more miles during the week. If I wanted to stay healthy, I'd take care of my body. Cause and effect. Simple math. Or so I thought.

My recent health crisis had pulled the rug out from under me. The math no longer added up. Though I had done all the right things, life had thrown me a set of circumstances that my capability couldn't overcome.

After the initial shock of the frightening seizure, I reached for God. Not that I had ignored God up until this point—He'd always been a distant, hazy figure. I trusted He'd created this earth, and me with good intentions and that He watched with kind benevolence from a distance. But with my recent health scare, I was *grasping* for Him. I no longer wanted a distant God. Not at all. I wanted—no, *needed*—an intimate, hands-on God. A God who loved His people enough to humble Himself and come to earth. A God who would sacrifice all for that one lost sheep. A God whose awesome love reached into hearts and changed them with the call of His voice.

> You are my hiding place; you will protect me from trouble and surround me with songs of deliverance.
>
> —PSALM 32:7 (NIV)

That's the God I needed. That's the God I prayed to and longed for. And, true to His character, He did not let me down. After one particularly hard night, when I wondered if I would forever be haunted by these horrible headaches, He gave me a sweet assurance in the form of a vision. In it, I was curled in the palm of His mighty, capable hand. The folds of His skin cradled me, and I knew complete peace. I felt His love. I *knew* His love. After the second spinal procedure, my headaches disappeared. My grades steadied. Now, it seemed the hardest thing I would have to navigate was my complete lack of coordination in gym class. But if God had seen me through the last few months, surely, He wouldn't abandon me as I acclimated back to such a seemingly normal thing as a gym-class volleyball game.

To my chagrin, the player on the other side of the net lobbed the ball toward me, and I positioned myself beneath it. I hit it at just the right angle, successfully setting up one of my classmates in the front row to return it over the net.

I breathed a sigh of relief and glanced at the clock. Five minutes down, twenty-eight to go.

By the halfway point of the game, I had managed to hit a couple of balls and missed a handful of others. We switched sides of the court, and I once again positioned myself in the back corner. I groaned as the ball flew over the net, straight toward me. Anticipating the force of it, I stretched my arms in front of me.

But instead of the force of a volleyball, an explosion sounded above, akin to gunfire. I shrieked and ducked down, the ball forgotten. Shattering glass rippled around me, spraying the glossy wood of the gym floor. What on earth had happened?

The ball fell behind me, but it didn't matter. The game was the last thing anyone in the gym was thinking about. My peers rushed toward me.

"Heidi, are you OK?"

"Oh my goodness, that scared me so bad!"

"What was that?"

The gym teacher jogged over, staring up at the ceiling. "The light exploded."

I looked up to see that the commercial light 25 feet above me had indeed burst.

The teacher's gaze ran over me, scanning me for injury. "Did it hit you? Are you OK?"

"Nothing hit me," I said, standing from my huddled position on the gym floor, visibly shaken as I brushed the sides of my arms, searching for some unfelt injury. But no, there wasn't a scratch on my skin. "I'm OK."

One of my friends pointed to the glass around me. "Look. A perfect circle."

I blinked. She was right. Surrounding me lay shards of ragged, broken glass, a complete halo a foot around my feet. I studied the space between me and the glass, a buffer of invisible protection.

> I give them eternal life, and they shall never perish; no one will snatch them out of my hand.
>
> —JOHN 10:28 (NIV)

"I think you have a guardian angel," another girl said.

My bottom lip trembled, and I tried to hold back grateful tears. As we left the court and the janitor came in to clean up the mess of broken glass, I marveled at God's perfect protection. Not only had He guided me through my recent health struggles, drawing me closer to Him than ever before, but here He still was, protecting me in the everyday course of normal life. His almighty hand and ever-watching eye were on all the details of my days—from the smaller things like homework and headaches to the bigger challenges of grand mal seizures and exploding glass.

My Baby's Shield
Kristen Paris

One, two, three. I counted my children coming out of the locker rooms. My exhaustion threshold had been reached, and counting to three was about all I felt I could manage. I buckled our preschool-aged son, Gage, into his booster seat and noticed that he had grown nearly as tall as his booster's hard, wing-like sides. Before long, he'd be using a regular seatbelt like his sisters. Wow! Time was passing too quickly.

As I started the van and pulled out of the parking lot, I glanced briefly at our two daughters. Their hair still dripped water from the hasty showers they'd taken after swim practice. They looked tired but were contentedly reading while our son played with a toy. They were my world: my reason for getting up each morning, and my own personal three-ring circus.

Mentally plotting out the rest of the week, I noticed traffic slowing through a construction zone in front of me. Suddenly, a harsh wind kicked up, sending dirt and debris swirling madly around our van. The realization cut through my brain fog: we were in the middle of a dust devil.

Jolted to alertness, I stopped in the middle of the freeway, terrified. The van rocked and shook as the whirlwind engulfed us, its roar drowning out all other sound—even our own voices. It was like being trapped in an alien world. Everything familiar had disappeared. Knowing I had no control over the situation and was helpless to protect my children, I prayed anxiously, *Lord, please protect these little ones.*

A sharp crack sounded, and then the buffeting dirt cleared as quickly as it had started.

Just as the air cleared enough for us to start forward again, my son's nerve-rattling scream pierced the air. He wasn't one to make a commotion. I glanced back over my right shoulder. Everything looked fine. Three kids and no blood. As long as he wasn't hurt, whatever was bothering him could be resolved after we got out of the area. I turned my attention back to the road ahead, but his cries intensified.

"Mom!" my younger daughter shouted.

"What? He seems fine," I responded, trying to safely navigate the freeway ahead.

> "Let the beloved of the LORD rest secure in him, for he shields him all day long."
>
> —DEUTERONOMY 33:12 (NIV)

"The window!" our oldest chimed in. "Look at the window."

I glanced over my other shoulder to see a web of crushed glass curtaining the left side of our van, barely holding together. My blood ran cold. *What just happened?* My exhaustion was overcome by reserves of strength and energy from outside of myself. I carefully eased over to the shoulder of the road.

Glass wasn't cascading out of the window—yet—so I took the offramp as gently as I could, again praying, *Lord, please, don't let that glass fly everywhere. Protect these children, and give me wisdom to stop if that window is going to cave in.*

"Close your eyes," I ordered, just in case the glass gave way.

Once off the freeway, I crawled into the back seat to unbuckle my distraught son, and examined the damage as I comforted him.

The front window panel on his side of the car had a small round hole, almost like a bullet hole, with cracks extending outward. The head protection panel of our son's booster seat showed a small dent. Further back, the next window panel was completely shattered into a hopeless mass of glass shards. The blood froze in my veins as I recognized the nearly fatal danger we'd just been through.

A small stone, whipped through the air by the powerful winds, must have shot through our window, hit the narrow wing protecting my son's head in his booster seat, and bounced. On the rebound, it had enough power left to shatter the back window. How on earth had it been stopped by that little strip of hard plastic, yet still ejected out through the glass window? It just wasn't possible.

After calling for help, I clutched our son close, as though he was still in danger of being ripped from my life. Our girls cuddled up beside me despite the hot weather, and we waited for the tow truck. Now that the crisis was over, I could process the impact of what had—and more importantly, hadn't—happened. That head protection wing on the car seat was only a few inches wide. Without it guarding him, that rock would have hit our son squarely on the left temple. He had clearly been shielded by more than plastic—an inch or two farther forward, and the stone would have hit his forehead. Given the speed and force of such winds behind it, there's no doubt that Gage wouldn't be here today without God's precise protection. Only foresight and strength beyond human capacity could have stopped that sudden, random dust devil from being fatal.

"Thank You, Lord. Thank You, thank You, thank You! You saved my children. I'm so grateful. Thank You for hearing my prayer and answering," I prayed, trembling, with tears running down my face.

With new wonder and a full heart, I gazed lovingly at the child in my arms. My girls also seemed to sense that a miracle had occurred and looked at their brother tenderly. His survival was important enough to our Heavenly Father that he was worth shielding. This child is a gift to me only for a time. He is God's forever. In awe, I pondered what God might have in store for him.

It was a reassurance I held in my heart throughout his childhood. As with any child, our son had plenty of troubles. There were seasons when I worried about his direction, his future, and his soul, especially during the difficult teen years. But God had claimed my son and watched over him. He'd spared his life when random chance would not have. I know that there must have been a reason.

> **He shielded him and cared for him; he guarded him as the apple of his eye.**
>
> —DEUTERONOMY 32:10 (NIV)

Now grown, our son has a heart for service. He worked as a lifeguard in high school, then as an EMT in a fire department as well as with campus safety through his college years. Today he is an Air Force officer who, off-duty, provides security at his church. A month ago, he and his beautiful, godly wife gave birth to a son. What a blessing we have watching him protect and provide for a family of his own! None of this would be possible had God not preserved his life when he was a preschooler. The protected became a protector.

Man's Bullets vs. God's Armor

Joe Fletcher

At the church I pastored in New York City, I conducted the services for the adults on Friday nights, while Larry and April Hendricks led our youth ministry. Our youth group was constantly trying to reach out to the teenagers in our neighborhood, and one of the ways we did so was through basketball. Our church's street, Morrison Avenue, is not an especially busy road for the Bronx, so when the weather was nice, our youth group would sometimes set up a portable basketball hoop in the street. When a car occasionally approached, the leaders made sure that the players got out of the way and let it pass. The basketball hoop was a magnet; teens would see the hoop, form a team, and play. Once the game was over, all the teens present were invited to come into our building for a meeting. Many of them would just go home at that point, but some would stay. Overall, it was a very effective strategy.

The basketball hoop was a little top-heavy and unsteady, so when our team set it up, they would put weights at the base of it to keep it from falling over. One night, when it was time to put the hoop away, one of the teens took the weights off the base. Before anyone could react, the hoop fell forward, hitting a 12-year-old boy in the head. The injury was serious enough that Larry called an ambulance. The young man lived across the street from our church. When his father realized what had happened, he immediately came out of his apartment building screaming, cursing, and demanding to speak to the pastor. I had been in the building conducting the prayer service. I didn't even know there was a problem outside until a teenager ran in and told me. When I came outside, a very angry father immediately began screaming and threatening me.

My first concern was the safety of our teenagers. I told Larry to take them all inside. He told them to go, but he stayed outside with me. Even when I insisted he leave, he said, "No, pastor, I'm staying outside!" He and I both sensed that this man was dangerous. It was the only time Larry ever defied me, and I was grateful!

I had been in a few tense ministry situations before, and I considered myself fairly adept at deescalating conflicts. But this time was different. Maybe it was fear, or maybe it was the Lord intervening, but when I tried to speak to this very angry father, all I could manage to say was, "God loves you." The more I said that, the angrier he seemed to become. Suddenly he walked quickly toward me. I braced myself, waiting for an assault. Then, inexplicably, he abruptly stopped, let out a weird laugh, shook his finger at me,

> **The LORD is my rock, my fortress and my deliverer; my God is my rock, in whom I take refuge, my shield and the horn of my salvation, my stronghold.**
>
> —PSALM 18:2 (NIV)

and backed up several steps. Shortly after that, he left to be with his son.

The injured young man was treated at the hospital and released that night. The incident should have been over, but it wasn't. Later that evening, I received a phone call from a member of our church who also lived very close to our church building. Someone had just shot several bullets into the front door of our church.

When I got to the church, the police were there, and the neighbors were outside talking to each other excitedly about the incident. Everyone knew what had happened. The angry father felt that he had not made his point strongly enough, so he shot several bullets through the front door of our church at around 11:00 p.m. Thankfully, no one had been in the building at that hour.

Several people in the neighborhood must have seen the incident. But when the police began to question the neighbors to try to find an eyewitness, everyone said they hadn't seen anything! The police brought the young man's father in for questioning, but he denied any involvement with the shooting. Beyond that, he wouldn't speak with them. This was not his first time in a police precinct. Since there were no witnesses, and there was not enough probable cause for the police to detain him or to get a warrant to search his apartment for a gun, they let him go.

Our daily church operation was small, and most weekdays I was in the building by myself. We did not have a parking lot, so I always parked on the street. After this incident, I was determined to keep doing my job and to continue to show up at the church every day. God had protected me before, and I knew that He would protect me again. Still, I never parked near the home of the shooter, and for several weeks I found myself nervously looking around when I walked from my car to the church building.

Shortly after the incident, Patterson, one of the leaders in our church, saw him on the street after the incident. Patterson struck up a conversation with him. He asked him how his son was doing. As they were speaking, Patterson found out that the father had completely misunderstood what had happened. He thought that his son had been injured because one of the other teens had bullied him. And he thought that our leaders had just stood by and let this happen. After Patterson explained to him what had actually happened, the father was calm and somewhat remorseful. Once Patterson told me about that conversation, I was able to breathe a little easier.

> Even though I walk through the darkest valley, I will fear no evil, for you are with me; your rod and your staff, they comfort me.
>
> —PSALM 23:4 (NIV)

I never saw the father again, but several weeks later, I learned that he and his family had moved out of the neighborhood. I was genuinely sad, knowing that we would not be able to minister to the young man who had been injured. But I was also relieved to know that this incident was now completely behind us.

As I look back at this experience, I realize that I will not fully understand all the details until I get to heaven. This man was capable of hurting me—or even killing me—but something stopped him. I am certain that he did not hesitate because he was afraid of me. I was no match for him physically, and I doubt that he was afraid of any long-term consequences of attacking me. If he were concerned about that, he wouldn't have shot several bullets into our church. Maybe something in his background or upbringing made him hesitate before striking the pastor of a church. Maybe God sent him a thought that made him hesitate. Or maybe, just maybe, God had sent His angels to make sure that no physical harm would come to me. In any case, however He did it, I knew that God had just saved me from harm once again.

The Day God Saved My Life

Robin Ayscue

I should not be here. That is an absolutely true statement. If God hadn't been watching out for me that day, you would not be reading these words. But here I am getting ahead of myself—let me tell you what happened.

I was driving down a familiar road, one I traveled several times a day. Suddenly, I caught a glimpse of a tractor trailer heading toward the intersection that I was about to enter. My light was green and his was red, yet the truck was barreling toward me with no sign of stopping. I immediately hit my brakes, but the pedal went straight to the floorboard of the car. The brakes were gone. I had an absolute death grip on that steering wheel as I prayed, "God, I'm going to hit him!"

There really are no words for what goes through your mind when you realize you are about to die. It was as though time stopped and eternity passed in those few seconds. I was just days shy of 50 years old. The faces of my family flashed before me as my heart said goodbye to them, believing I would never see any of them again on this side of eternity. I was sure that I was going to die, and in just a second I was going to see His Face, and leave all of this behind. The time was here; it was not like I planned, but it was getting ready to happen. All the longing for eternity, the waiting to see Him—it was happening, now. No time to make things right, no time to pray again, no time to love again, no time to serve Him again. It was over, finished. Eternity was here for me. Somehow there was enough time to think of that in just those few seconds. I was still holding on to the steering wheel for dear life, knowing I was about to die.

Then the presence of God, the Eternal One, the Maker of all the Universe, filled my car in those seconds I thought would be my last. He took over my arms and slowly turned that steering wheel so that my car rolled uphill to a stop in the middle of the intersection as the truck sped by. And there I sat. Still alive.

> "Go, stand in the temple courts," he said, "and tell the people all about this new life."
>
> —ACTS 5:20 (NIV)

I remember seeing faces of the people in cars that had stopped as they witnessed what was going to be a horrific accident. They were all white as a sheet. Some were already getting out of their cars to come and check on me. Somehow, I was able to gather myself enough so that, with help from the bystanders, I rolled the car into a nearby parking lot. I waved my thanks to my helpers. Then I started to shake uncontrollably.

I was in shock the rest of the day. I don't know if you have ever come this close to death and survived, but shock is the natural reaction, I guess. I know that I immediately made calls to my mama and my daughter, Ashley. And to work—I would not be going into my job that day.

That night, I went to church for Bible study. My heart was absolutely so full of God's praise that I felt it would explode if

I didn't tell what had happened to me just several hours before. Not only had God saved my life, but He had also been so very close to me in the car, and that changes you. Forever.

Thankfully, one of the first things they asked during the study was if anyone had a praise to share. I wept uncontrollably for the first time over the unbelievable miracle that I had experienced that day. In the Bible study, people were rejoicing with me. They, too, were praising God for saving my life that day. They offered me so much love; almost everyone in the room hugged me, which I desperately needed after facing death head on. Tears are rolling down my cheeks as I type this, just remembering the multitude of emotions that I was experiencing. God used those people—there were probably around seventy-five in that room that night—to minister to me and rejoice with me over the miracle that God had done in my life on that day. How I praise Him for leading me there, as He knew I would need their love and support after such a life-altering event.

> **Praise the Lord. Praise God in his sanctuary; praise him in his mighty heavens. Praise him for his acts of power; praise him for his surpassing greatness.**
>
> —PSALM 150:1–2 (NIV)

Over the next few days, my spirit walked through what would have happened if I had died. I thought about who would be planning my funeral and what would they choose for it. I knew the funeral would have been on Saturday. I wondered who would have come. I could not seem to stop dwelling on this near-death experience.

I did not sleep for two solid nights after my close call. But as word got out about what had happened, so many wonderful friends and extended family reached out to me to hear what God had done and rejoice that God had chosen to let me live. The beautiful presence that had filled my car still seemed so very close to me. I simply could not get away from Him. And I never wanted to.

This incredible experience removed all fear of death from me. I know that no matter what happens to me or what pain I may endure in this life, when my time comes, He will be there. He will take me. He will bring me His Peace.

Always by Our Side
Linda Marie

The sanctuary at our neighborhood church was filled with young people from surrounding states, there to attend a youth conference. Their enthusiasm was contagious, and my friend and I were uplifted and inspired by the program.

Two days later I was at urgent care, and less than a week later, I was in the hospital. I had Covid-19. The day I was admitted, my lung collapsed, and my hospital room filled with commotion and people. Someone gave me a shot of morphine, and I could hear the doctor giving a nurse instructions as she cut into my chest to insert a tube to inflate my lung.

Please, God, help me, I prayed, and said the Lord's Prayer out loud until I passed out. I'm not sure how long I was asleep, but when I woke up, I had a nasal cannula—a very thin tube several feet long that stretched from my nose to an oxygen port in the wall. I was on 100 percent oxygen.

I slept a lot and could barely eat. In the middle of the second day, the doctor came in and said that I was not getting any better. He wanted my permission to revive me with a defibrillator, should my heart stop, and permission to put me on a ventilator if needed. I had not filled out any hospital directives or a living will. I can still remember sitting there, looking at him, chilled at how matter-of-fact he sounded about the possibility that I might die.

That was the point when I believe God gave me extra strength and discernment. I was sick and so tired, but I knew I did not want to be put on a ventilator under any circumstance. I had a friend who had been on a ventilator and then died, and had heard about the same happening to others. I told him that if my heart stopped, they could use a defibrillator, but I would not agree to be put on a ventilator. He told me that if things got worse, the ventilator could save my life. I still said no and was adamant. I would not give consent.

> And the peace of God, which transcends all understanding, will guard your hearts and your minds in Christ Jesus.
>
> —PHILIPPIANS 4:7 (NIV)

The next morning the nurse came in and said they were transferring me to another hospital. They put me on a gurney and into an ambulance. I was so weak that I slept through the trip. I was admitted to a rehab hospital, where, I found out later, most of the patients were terminal. I really believe the doctors at the first hospital did not expect me to survive, but because the doctors and nurses at the rehab hospital took such good care of me, I lived.

I was constantly being wheeled to X-ray, having my blood drawn, or taking medication. The nurses were like God's angels on earth. This was during the early stages of the Covid pandemic, when no one was sure of anything about the disease. These nurses and doctors were willing to potentially lay down their lives for their patients by caring for them. The nurses on my floor were friendly and chatty. When they came to my room, they would share stories of what was going on outside of the hospital or about their family lives. I have to admit, I was not very lively at the time. I just listened in between sleeping off and on through the days and nights. My family was out of state, but even if they were in town, they would not have been allowed to see me. They called the head nurse each day to check on my progress, then relayed the information to my friends.

The only time I was able to get out of bed was to go to the bathroom or to sit in the chair beside the bed to eat. There was an alarm on the bed because of the fall risk, and I had to call a nurse each time I did any of these things. Having always been so independent, this was very humbling and hard to accept. For one of the only times in my life, I was faced with a situation where sheer willpower was not enough to conquer. I had to completely depend on other people—and God.

> **Greater love has no one than this: to lay down one's life for one's friends.**
>
> —JOHN 15:13 (NIV)

I wish that I could say that during this quiet time I prayed deep prayers to God, but I was in some kind of a daze. I was going through the motions of living with little thought or animation. And yet, God really blessed me. I remember that I felt His presence with me continually. At times when I should have felt great physical pain—like when they inserted the chest tube or later when they removed it—I felt calm, and it did not hurt. When I could have been afraid, He graced me with a peace that was not understandable under the circumstances. I didn't worry about whether I would live or die. I didn't worry about

GOD'S GIFT OF TASTE
— Kim Taylor Henry —

AS JESUS WALKED through crowds that had come to see him, they "almost crushed him" (Luke 8:42, NIV). Jesus did not respond to those touches. Then came a single touch on his cloak's edge, to which he responded immediately. A woman who had been bleeding for years had reached out in faith, believing Jesus could heal her. And heal her Jesus did, for He recognized and valued her touch as a touch of genuine faith, not of curiosity, eagerness, or mere presence. Touch can speak, as this woman's touch did to Jesus. It told Him she fully believed in Him. That is the kind of faith to which He always responds.

---

the bills or if I would lose my job. Somehow, deep inside I felt a calm assurance that everything would be all right. I believe that this peace was due, in large part, to the many prayers that friends and family were offering up for me each day. They stood in the gap for me when I was too sick to pray for myself.

I felt the Holy Spirit leading me to do things that were very difficult but were necessary for my recovery. One of those things was to drag myself out of bed whenever a nurse brought meals. It would take me a long time to finish eating, because even with all the oxygen I was receiving, I was short of breath and exhausted as I ate. Yet I was compelled to take care of myself in this way.

Two-and-a-half weeks later, when I was finally able to go to physical therapy, I could barely walk. It was painful, and

I needed a nurse beside me as I went, but I pushed to do it. Gradually they reduced the amount of oxygen I was being given, but I was told that when released I would need to be on oxygen at home, possibly permanently. By this time, I was feeling well enough to join my friends and family in prayer, and I asked God to please heal my lungs and let me breathe freely.

He answered those prayers. After almost a month in two different hospitals, I left the rehab hospital without any supplemental oxygen. At my most recent office visit, my doctor said my lungs sound completely clear.

I don't think I truly understood the power of prayer until this experience, but now I do. And since that time, I know that God is always by my side.

The Man with Nine Lives
John Peterson, as told to Wendy Lynne Smith

As the owner of a roofing company, I encountered danger every day. From walking on steep pitches and climbing an extension ladder to building decks and trimming trees, it was all part of the job. I have always been thankful my wife and kids covered me in prayer. My wife hosts a weekly prayer meeting, and every day, she intercedes for my safety and well-being. It's a good thing she does, because recently there have been three different occasions where the Lord stepped in to ensure my safety.

The first was an ordinary afternoon, and I was putting composition shingles on a one-story home. I didn't notice it, but someone must have bumped the ladder while I was on the roof, so it leaned at a slight angle on the metal gutter. When I put my foot on the ladder to descend and get another bundle of roof tiles, the ladder slipped.

I fell like a rock, landing on my hands and knees, and I heard a slapping sound as my palms hit the concrete sidewalk. My guardian angels must have cushioned the fall and softened the blow, because even a one-story fall could have resulted in a head injury or a broken back. Instead, I simply got up, fixed the ladder, and went back to work.

A new day brought another project; this time I was building a deck on the back of the second story of our two-story house. As I stood on a ladder, cutting off an end piece, I lost my footing and fell. I was holding an open skill saw in my hand, the spinning blade a silver flash. My tool belt was loaded with heavy metal objects. And I was free falling.

I focused on holding onto that whirling saw, my arm stretched out as far away from my body as possible. The hammer flew off of the tool belt and, by a stroke of random chance, landed in a standing position on the grass. My head bounced off the tool, hitting my eye hard as I landed on the grass. The right side of my face pulsated with pain, and I thought my eyeball had exploded. I lay still for a moment—just breathing. Taking stock.

But then I opened my eyes, and I could see! Eyes are flexible. I realized that I had instinctively closed my eyes, and my eyelid protected my eye, while the glasses I had been wearing had slipped away so that the hammer didn't smash the glass into my skin.

> **The LORD protects the unwary; when I was brought low, he saved me.**
>
> —PSALM 116:6 (NIV)

I groaned as I pushed my aching body into a sitting position and stood up. I stumbled into the house to look in the mirror and check out my throbbing eye.

"What happened?" my wife exclaimed in dismay. A retired baker and cake decorator, she set the spatula down abruptly on the kitchen counter, causing gooey batter to splatter on the floor. Dozens of cupcakes lined the counter, and the aroma of vanilla and chocolate was heavenly.

Grass clung to my clothes. My glasses were broken, and a large black bruise was beginning to form under my eye. My caring wife rushed to the first-aid kit and pulled out the antiseptic and bandages, but there was no broken skin and nothing to be done except to put a cold cloth on my face to ward off swelling. So, after enjoying an ice-cold drink and a couple of delicious cupcakes, I went back to work.

Thank you, Heavenly Father! I praised. *That was a close one.* Both of those accidents had the potential for great injury, and yet, God—in His infinite wisdom—faithfully protected me time and time again. What I didn't know was that the worst mishap was yet to come.

There was an enormous cedar tree shading my daughter-in-law's backyard, where she enjoyed growing lettuce, tomatoes, strawberries, and beautiful flowers in raised beds. She and my son had labored over their garden, cultivating and tending each sweet stalk. I offered to prune a thick tree branch that had grown out over the garden, giving it too much shade.

> **The LORD watches over all who love him.**
>
> —PSALM 145:20 (NIV)

Again, I was on a ladder. In order to reach the part of the branch I wanted to cut off, I leaned the ladder against the branch itself. I thought it would be safe because the ladder was on a part of the branch that was closer to the trunk. What a terrible mistake!

Crack! As the end of the branch I was cutting snapped, it dropped to the ground. But the part that was still attached to the tree was now much lighter, and it rebounded abruptly, sending the ladder and pruning tools flying. I catapulted into the air and plunged 10 feet to the ground, dropping like a dead weight on top of the ladder.

"Oomph!" I grunted as the rungs bit into my ribs. I lay there for a moment, wondering if anything was broken.

"Are you OK?" I heard the words, but they sounded far away. I glimpsed shoes as my family gathered around my prone body. After mentally checking over my limbs, I decided to try to stand up. I muscled my way up and crawled off the ladder. Then I stood up and walked over to a patio chair.

"I thought you were dead," my wife gasped. She covered her face, tears filling her eyes as she reached out to hold my hand. I clasped hers tightly so she would know I still had some strength left.

"Should I call 911?" my daughter-in-law called out, phone in hand.

"Let us know what we can do," my son said.

"I think I'm OK," I answered slowly, amazed at the truth of it. God's loving arms had caught me again, sparing me serious injury or worse, death.

"Is your garden all right?" I asked. "I hope the plants didn't get smashed."

My wife chuckled through her tears, and she smiled tremulously. "The garden's fine. Everything's fine. We're just concerned about you!"

But other than a couple of bruised ribs, I knew I would be fine too. I'd just survived the biggest fall I'd ever had. Yet I would walk away—as I had the two times before—whole in body, mind, and spirit, from an accident that could have resulted in a debilitating injury. God's constant protection for me was evidence of His loving care and the way that He answers our prayers.

Transformation is a process, and as life happens there are tons of ups and downs. It's a journey of discovery—there are moments on mountaintops and moments in deep valleys of despair.

—Rick Warren

CHAPTER 2

God Travels with Us

Into the Storm 46
    Shannon Leach

The Secret of the Silver Olds 54
    Roberta Messner

Even When We Run 59
    Elsa Kok Colopy

I Gave God One More Day, and He Made a Way 62
    Elizabeth Renicks

40 Minutes 69
    Mary Vee

A Sudden Halt 78
    Robin T. Jennings

Dry in the Rain 83
    Christel Owoo

On the Road with God 89
    Sandra Ardoin

God Is in the Details 95
    Tina Wanamaker

Into the Storm
Shannon Leach

I parked the rental van in the hotel lot, pushed the button to silence the engine, and laid my head back on the seat. As I turned the rearview mirror in my direction, I took a deep breath and sighed. An afternoon of crying had left my face swollen, and despite only being on the road for a few hours, I felt exhausted. My mind drifted back to my foster mother's face as I kneeled beside her and said goodbye. Pulling myself away from her side and walking out that door was the hardest thing I had ever done. She had only been in hospice for a few weeks but was fading fast, and I did not know if I would ever see her again on this earth.

This woman was more to me than just a foster mom. More than a stranger who opened her home to a struggling teen. She was my rock, my prayer warrior, my cheerleader, and advocate. I could not bear to process what my life would look like without her. I felt the heaviness settle upon me as I headed back to my boys and my husband and my job. Three days with her was not enough. No amount of time would have been enough for me to say goodbye. As I had lingered with her for one more moment, and another and another, something had nudged me, telling me it was time to go.

Since I left her side, I had driven three-and-a-half hours clutching tightly to the steering wheel, fighting against the brutal Kansas wind and my worries. I begged through tears and bargained through pain, crying out to God to be with me and heal my heart for what I knew was coming. By the time I reached Kansas City, I knew I would have to stop driving. My mind and body were emotionally and physically drained.

I debated whether I should keep going, knowing my boys needed me back home, and my husband's fiftieth birthday was tomorrow. I never expected to make the drive in one day, but I had planned to get farther than this. However, when I saw the familiar hotel I had stayed at on my way out 3 days before, my soul cried out for rest. Everything about this trip had been foreign to me, from the reason to the rental, and that one second of recognition felt like shelter in the storm.

> **He stilled the storm to a whisper; the waves of the sea were hushed.**
>
> —PSALM 107:29 (NIV)

My husband understood. "I've got this," he said when I called him. "You stop and get some sleep. But get going in the morning. They're saying the weather is supposed to be bad tomorrow," he cautioned.

Within minutes, I had the room keycard in hand. I dropped my bags beside the bed, grabbed the remote and clicked on The Weather Channel. As I walked into the bathroom to wash my face, words like "high-risk forecast" and "very active storm pattern" drifted in from the other room. I made a mental note to check the radar in the morning after breakfast, then crawled under the crisp white duvet, not bothering to change or to turn the television off, and was asleep within minutes.

"This is a particularly dangerous situation."

My eyes fluttered open at the words. I squinted at the ceiling as I tried to recall where I was. Oh, yes. That hotel. I grabbed my glasses and glanced at my phone to check the time; it was almost 7:00 a.m.

"If you are in a rental and you did not get the damage protection, now might be a great time to add that on," the on-screen announcer continued.

I sat straight up in the bed and stared at the television. *I am in a rental. And I didn't get the damage protection.* It only took one look at the forecast radar to get me moving.

"This area of the mid-south, especially this area around Memphis, looks to be one of the two areas likely to have a severe outbreak of tornadoes."

I live around Memphis. That's me. I moved to the bathroom and started gathering up the few things I had unpacked and threw them in a bag, forgoing my usual organized packing. I pulled my hair under a hat and stacked my bags by the door.

"Potential timing looks to be around 3:00 p.m."

I ticked off the hours in my head. It would take 8 hours to get from Kansas City to my home even if I didn't stop. *There is no way I would make it, even if I leave right now.* But I had to try. I thought of my younger son and how terrified he was of storms. Although grown, his autism meant he didn't handle scary situations well and my husband would not be home until after 5 p.m. This wasn't good.

Soon I was loading my bags in the van and setting the GPS to home. I glared at the estimated arrival time on the screen. It read 3:15 p.m. I started rethinking the damage protection, but that meant I would have to find a rental location where I could add it on, which would take more time. Even worse, from where I was, there was no way around the storms. The forecast predicted the line of storms would reach from Illinois to Mississippi. I would be driving straight south for more than 8 hours. Right into the weather.

I decided to risk the time delay and seek out the insurance. Minutes later, I pulled onto the interstate, GPS set for the nearest location for the rental car company I was using.

More than an hour later, I pulled out of another rental car lot, frustrated. The first location I'd tried was still closed, and the second one could not help. Since I had rented the van at an airport, I had to add the protection at an airport. I glanced at the sky. Low-hanging clouds had replaced yesterday's blue skies, but there had been no rain so far. Now I had to decide whether to stop in St. Louis—the nearest airport along my route, though it was still three-and-a-half hours from Kansas City—to get the damage protection. *Lord, I don't see a way out of this, so I need you to help me through it.* I scolded myself for stopping at the hotel so far from home. But then I remembered why I had to, and the tears started over again. *Lord, I need you here with me right now. What do I do?*

> "Have I not commanded you? Be strong and courageous. Do not be afraid; do not be discouraged, for the LORD your God will be with you wherever you go."
>
> —JOSHUA 1:9 (NIV)

He answered through my husband. "You might be OK," he said when I called. "It's pushed back until after four now. Sounds like it is slowing down some. But I would get that protection. They're predicting hail and probably tornadoes." As he described the changes in the timing, I knew God was hearing my prayers. It made the decision to stop in St. Louis for the damage protection much easier, but there was still no time to waste. As I sat at the rental counter in St. Louis, I continued to feel the urgency. That storm was still coming.

I walked back to the van, now worried that this stop had taken too long. Suddenly, I felt the first raindrops on my arm. I climbed in, looking through the windshield at the building clouds, my anxiety building along with them. I could not shake the weight of the last 24 hours, walking through an emotional storm just to drive into a physical one. *God, stay with me, please.*

Town after town went by as I headed south. The updates continued. Reports of school dismissal at 1:30 p.m. and businesses closing showed the threat was still very real. My husband called to tell me he was coming home early as well. I breathed a sigh of relief, knowing the boys wouldn't be home alone. God was still hearing my prayers.

The next four-and-a-half hours were a blur as I shifted between the GPS and the radar, recounting the minutes each time. I was always shocked that the storm that was so close the last time I had looked had still not reached me yet. It was almost as if it was waiting for me to make it home.

Finally, I pulled into the driveway a little after 5 p.m. I grabbed what I could carry and hurried into the house. I laid the keys to the rental van on the island and noticed the radar was already playing on every television. My boys rushed into the kitchen with hugs and words of welcome home. Hugs felt more important to me right now as I thought of my mom. My husband gave me a quick kiss on the cheek and offered to go unload the rest of my bags as my younger son, already anxious, gave me a play-by-play of the weather reports.

"And there is a tornado someplace in Arkansas. Wynn. Yes, Wynn. It did a lot of damage. They said it is coming this way," he continued.

I started unpacking as he told me all I would ever need to know about storms for the next 20 minutes, following me from room to room as I put things away. I glanced out the window and noticed the wind picking up.

Reports of multiple tornadoes across the river blared from the television screen as the sudden screeching of our phones startled us all. The weather warning confirmed our worst fear: a tornado on the ground and heading right for us. There was no more time for unpacking. We rushed to the bedroom closet, more well-practiced at this routine than we should have been for living in Tennessee. Growing up in Kansas, heading to the basement was normal. I never had expected to shelter so often in this part of the world. I hoped this would be a false alarm.

It wasn't.

We listened to the television describe the damage this EF-3 tornado had already caused, and tried to not panic as I heard them mention this was the same tornado that hit Wynn,

> But let all who take refuge in you be glad; let them ever sing for joy. Spread your protection over them, that those who love your name may rejoice in you.
>
> —PSALM 5:11 (NIV)

Arkansas, killing four people. It had been on the ground for over an hour already. Five minutes away. Four minutes away. Now three. The meteorologist's countdown went silent as the power went out.

"Mama, what do we do now?" my older son asked. I stared at him, trying not to show my fear.

"We pray," I said. "We pray hard right now." I grabbed their hands, and we prayed. We prayed for protection. We prayed for safety. We prayed for God to take the storm away. The sound of things hitting the side of the house filled the silence in between. We braced for impact.

The impact never came.

A few minutes later, my husband stepped out and started walking around the house, much to my protest. I heard him go out the back door, and I demanded he get back inside. Instead, he yelled for me to come out.

I stepped out of the closet and saw light pouring through the bedroom window. Surprised to see daylight, I followed my husband outside, astounded when I saw a blue sky. In the distance toward town, the sky was swirling and black.

"Where did it go?" I asked, looking at my husband.

A voice from behind me answered. "God was in the closet, and He took it away," said my younger son.

I looked back at the sky. *Not just in the closet. He has been here all day.* But it was more than that. Not just today, but all the time. He is always standing with me, both in the storms and in clear weather. The only difference was today, I had the blessing of seeing Him working through one after another "it just so happened" moments.

And there were so many of those.

GOD'S GIFT OF SIGHT
— Kimberly Shumate —

IN 1 SAMUEL 3:18 (NIV) Eli says, "He is the Lord; let him do what is good in his eyes." Sometimes what is good in the eyes of one person is less favorable in the eyes of another. It's all in how we look at it. Yet it is the blackest storm clouds and sheets of rain that most fully saturate the ground for a future harvest. When the tempest has fled and all is quiet again, you'll see God's gifts in His soil of new opportunity. When it seems like He is raining challenges down on you, He is preparing His best for your future.

We would learn later the EF-3 tornado that had been on the ground for 73 miles dissipated back into the clouds barely 3 miles from our house. We would hear of the fourteen tornadoes that touched down that day in our area, including the one that destroyed schools and hundreds of homes only minutes away. And we would never forget hundreds of stories in which people had experienced just enough time to get to safety in the storm. Many talked about the coincidence and how lucky they were to be right where they were. But I knew it was because God was there with them, too.

The Secret of the Silver Olds

Roberta Messner

I rang the bell for my weekly visit at Madison Park Healthcare, where the past seemed more alive than the present. Several of the church ladies from my childhood were residents there. Photographs and memories would fill my hour in Dorothy's room. We'd been perusing the pages of the faux-wood-grained albums in her bookcase. She was asking today for the one labeled "CAMP," where faces I'd long forgotten were stuck to yellowed cellophane. "This'll take you back," Dorothy said, pointing to four smiling, apron-clad ladies from church camp who'd shopped for the pancake fixings we had for breakfast and the marshmallows we roasted after dark.

I dusted off my heart, settling in on the side of her narrow bed and allowing the photos to turn back time. There was a much younger Dorothy, along with Maxine, Myrna, and Nell. The quartet of ladies had formed a marching band after our camp meals. Dorothy led the parade as pots and pans and metal spatulas and spoons clanged out a melody for cheering kids. Smiling Nell playing a silent melody on a pretend violin.

"Nell never said much," I recalled, my hands brushing the image of the petite, serene lady. Nell Creasy had first claimed my attention in the white clapboard sanctuary at Seventh

Avenue Baptist. I had a front row-seat for watching the pianist's flying fingers and the music coming from golden satin choir robes. Nell's beautiful singing was an expression of her beautiful, genuine faith.

But Nell didn't truly change my life until much later, when I bought her car. Her silver Olds had entered my life at a time when I was desperate to believe in God's protection and provision—and it showed me just that, in a way I never could have imagined.

I snuggled into the little bed beside Dorothy and began to tell her all about it. In the 1980s, I'd taken a sideline job as a magazine photo stylist and needed a more dependable vehicle to travel to homes around the country. I couldn't afford a new car, much less the luxury models that Superior Cadillac and Oldsmobile offered. One afternoon I was running errands when balloons lured me into a used-vehicle lot. A silver Oldsmobile Cutlass Supreme pulled me toward it like a magnet.

An unexplainable urge to take it for a test drive consumed me. "Grab the keys to the Creasy car," the salesman called to a coworker. He spoke in a confidential whisper I assumed was a sales chat-up. "Those Creasy cars are really special." His voice was oddly earnest. Convincing. When I took it out on the highway for the test drive, I felt secure. Cared for. Comfortable and comforted. It was more than its low-mileage, new-car smell and velour seats. There was something special about this vehicle I couldn't explain. I bought Nell's car on the spot.

> For he will command his angels concerning you to guard you in all your ways.
>
> —PSALM 91:11 (NIV)

A day or so after I signed on the dotted line, my friend Jesse and I planned a Saturday of junking. Jesse had a fun gift for my new wheels, a bumper sticker that said, *This car stops at all yard sales.* We'd chuckled at the thought. But what happened was far from funny. "While parked on a hill, the emergency brake failed, and the car started rolling backward—straight toward the crowd," I told Dorothy, the memory still giving me shivers.

It should have been a disaster. I'd never forget how screaming shoppers held on to each other as Nell's Olds zigzagged through a rose garden without taking a single petal. But then, before the car could reach the tables—let alone one of the terrified bystanders—it stopped. Just came to a sudden halt, as if on command.

Everyone around us was staring in shock. Finally, a man holding on to a tool chest for dear life proclaimed, "Only one explanation—angelic protection!"

I couldn't help but agree. I'd gone to church eight times a week before I was even born. And I'd memorized the scriptures about God giving his angels charge over us. But until that Saturday, I'd never seen evidence of it.

After that, I really noticed the feeling of protection that came over me whenever I got into that car. When I drove to one of my styling gigs, it was just me and my props, like before. But I was never alone. Or afraid. Or shy. I invited new friends in states I'd never visited before out to dinner. It seemed to shelter them as well.

One evening as dusk was turning into darkness, I got a flat tire on a potholed country road. I had no idea where I was, and I started to panic. Then what appeared to be a motorcycle gang pulled up beside Nell's Oldsmobile. I was terrified that they were Hell's Angels and that I was about to get robbed or worse. But God was watching over me that night, and it turned out they just wanted to help. Two bearded guys in black leather jackets fixed my flat while one kept me company on the velour passenger seat. The other fellow fetched me Slim Jims and Fritos and an ice-cold Mountain Dew from their private stash. Those bikers were angels, all right.

I drove Nell's silver Olds for 12 years. Except for that fateful flat, it never needed more than routine maintenance. When I gifted it to a family member who drove it off to college, the story was the same—they always felt protected whenever they traveled in that car.

Hearing my story now, Dorothy smiled. "I'm not surprised at any of this," she said, patting my knee. She revealed the Olds' secret: Nell's faith-filled tradition whenever she traded in vehicles. "Before she handed over the keys, Roberta, she said a prayer for the angels to stay."

> **They are new every morning; great is your faithfulness.**
>
> —LAMENTATIONS 3:23 (NIV)

There's even more to the secret of the silver Olds, dear reader. While I still had it, I not only felt protected, but I was inspired with a deeper urge to take care of others. I stocked the trunk with thick woolen socks and sweaters and kept an eye out along the way for folks who might need them. Blankets, too. I met the nicest folks on my travels, many of whom were experiencing homelessness and very difficult times.

The influence of the silver Olds didn't stop when I changed vehicles. I still carry items that I can give to others, even if it's as simple as having an extra umbrella on rainy days to share with someone who got caught without one. And to this very day, every morning before my feet hit the floor, I pray a Roberta paraphrase of Nell's angelic invitation: "Send me to them, Lord, and them to me. Teach me to trust when I find some who might need my help and to know them when you send them."

Even When We Run
Elsa Kok Colopy

It was a lovely spring afternoon when my little girl decided to run away.

It all began when 11-year-old Savannah woke up feeling a little off. No fever, just an ache or two. She moaned. She groaned a bit. And then with a big sigh, she proclaimed that she just didn't feel like she could go to school.

Now Savannah is not one to make up these things, so we let her stay home. But miracle of miracles, just an hour or two later, she started feeling better. Her brother had a track meet in the afternoon, and she was certain she could make it to that.

"Oh no," I said. "House rule, remember? If you stay home from school, no other activities that day."

"But I'm better," she protested.

Nope.

"But I'll go to school right now." She crossed her arms and raised her voice. "I want to go to school right now."

I was pretty sure that because she called in sick already, she wouldn't be able to attend at all. I shook my head. "No, sweetheart. No school for you today. Hopefully you will feel better tomorrow, and you can go to school then."

It may have been the busy weekend we'd had, or the late night a few days prior, or maybe even pre-teen moodiness, but our little one had a major meltdown. She scrunched up her beautiful face, pursed her lips, and stomped her feet. "I knew it! You don't even care about me," she yelled. And with that she headed to the front door. "I'm walking to school, and no one can stop me."

Alrighty then.

I know my girl and the way she is wired. Responding harshly in moments like this would backfire into an hours-long meltdown. So I walked out the door and followed her.

She was still in her jammies and had no shoes on, but she was determined to walk the 15 miles to her elementary school.

She'd walked about a half-mile when I reminded her of some construction up ahead. "You'll probably have to go in the other direction. The sidewalk is broken up over there."

I'm so very helpful.

She turned and walked in the other direction, and I stayed about 15 yards back.

> **Where can I go from your Spirit? Where can I flee from your presence? If I go up to the heavens, you are there; if I make my bed in the depths, you are there.**
>
> —PSALM 139:7–8 (NIV)

I pulled out my phone and turned on some worship music. I had to laugh out loud when the next song began to play: "Where Can I Go from Your Presence?"

The chorus played as I drew up right behind her, matching her step for step. She picked up her speed. As did I. She might have been running, but I wasn't going to let her run alone.

Finally she slowed a bit, and I came up beside her. "I really want to go to school, Mom. I feel better."

"Well, since you are talking to me in a reasonable tone, we can certainly ask, and if they say yes, you can put some clothes and shoes on, and I'll give you a ride. If they say no, you have to honor that."

She nodded.

We walked a bit farther and began circling back to the house. I spoke again. "The only thing is, you have to apologize to me for yelling and for saying I don't care when you know that I love you with all my heart."

She stopped. Mumbled something. "What's that?" I said, "Peas are orange?"

She giggled and mumbled something else. "You like strange hamburgers?"

She laughed out loud. "I'm sorry, Mom," she said clearly.

"Oh," I said, laughing too. "I forgive you."

She hugged me close, and then we walked back to the house.

As I walked, I reflected on how I'm a lot like my 11-year-old daughter. Sometimes my childish heart wants to run away. From pain. From loss. From circumstances. From responsibility. And sometimes I *do* run, inside my heart. I dodge emotions, I circumvent the heartache. I run from intimacy with my God.

Then I'll sense Him. The warmth of His presence, the shadow of His love. It's definitely Him. My God. He follows a few steps behind, always present, protective—just waiting for me to turn and collapse into His arms.

When my girl "ran away" and walked down the street away from me, my love for her did not wane. It surged. I felt it fierce and strong. No way would she be able to run from it. Ever.

How much greater the love of my God who fashioned me, delights in me and gets me all the way to my core?

Even when I run.

I Gave God One More Day, and He Made a Way

Elizabeth Renicks

The wipers slashed back and forth across the windshield, firing rapidly but struggling to clear the deluge of water pouring from the sky. On high alert, I white-knuckled the steering wheel, leaning forward tensely, straining to see the road. My husband and two sons slept peacefully, unaware of the storm that swirled around us as I navigated our van through the unfamiliar, winding roads of a West Virginia interstate. As usual, I felt the weight of keeping everyone safe.

The naps and the storm had been going on for hours. It was the longest stretch of private, quiet time I had experienced in 7 days of travel. My thoughts were firing as rapidly as the windshield wipers. Emotions stuffed down all week were churning to the surface. The thunderous weather perfectly reflected the disorientation in my spirit. I prayed for discernment, but mostly wrestled with uncertainty and fear.

The previous Friday we had set out on a long-awaited family vacation. Just after putting the boys to bed in our hotel room, I had gotten a text. My younger brother Daniel had been taken to the ER with chest pains. Over the next hours, we learned he had suffered at least one heart attack and had significant blockages around his heart, requiring stents. The more we learned, the more we realized how miraculous it was he was alive. His bloodwork had revealed staggeringly high numbers, previously undetected. A1C over 13. Cholesterol over 600. Blockages in particularly dangerous locations. Doctors called him a medical miracle. We were all thankful that he had survived.

Now, driving through the rain, I was faced with choices I had put off thinking about all week. We had been encouraged to carry on with our vacation because Daniel was getting good care, surrounded by other family. On this return trip, we would have our chance to see him. If we spent the night with my sister tonight as planned, we could visit Daniel tomorrow.

I had begun waffling about this plan almost as soon as it was made. My father-in-law had faced triple-bypass heart surgery just three months earlier. With my homeschooled kids in tow, I had been regularly involved in his care over weeks of transition from hospital to rehab to home. We had all felt the strain of disrupted routines and drained reserves as he weathered months of complications and recovery. Now my brother was dealing with similar issues. It was too much.

> **I sought the LORD, and he answered me; he delivered me from all my fears.**
>
> —PSALM 34:4 (NIV)

The vacation that was to have allowed space for restoration from our months of caregiving had now become a new battleground. I wasn't sure I could get close to another catastrophic health issue so soon. Neither my emotions nor my faith felt up to the challenge. It was one thing for my elderly father-in-law to have cardiac issues. It was quite another for my younger brother to have a heart attack at the age of 43. The physical distance between me and Daniel kept this new reminder of suffering and death at a remove. Each mile I drove pushed me closer to having to make a choice about whether to stop and see him, to let the anxieties and fears come back into the forefront of my life again.

In the home we grew up in there was a subtle but strong emphasis on staving off ill-health or suffering. Vigilance was key. This manifested itself in hundreds of parental injunctions to "be careful." Mom refused to let my brother play football because it was too dangerous. We couldn't ride the neighbor's motorcycles or jump on a friend's trampoline. Our living room end tables were stacked with back issues of *Prevention* magazine. Taped inside every kitchen cabinet door were clipped-out magazine articles on better eating strategies or the benefit of vitamins. The message was everywhere: *You must take care*. Staying safe apparently rested completely on our shoulders.

A place of constant reminders to be wary of the world's dangers is where fearful hearts are born and nurtured. The atmosphere I breathed as a child manifested itself in anxieties and exhaustion in my adult life. Hypervigilance about health in my childhood home was perplexing, too, as it stood in contrast to Mom's faith in Christ and His provision in other areas of life. I found contradictions between Mom's expressed faith and her lived actions. If we trusted God, why did we have to work so hard to protect ourselves? Deeper still, it had left me with a woefully incomplete theology about suffering and death. I had been trained to avoid suffering and pain as I grew up. As an adult I had adopted an avoidance strategy about painful places where I had few answers.

Daniel's heart attack had opened floodgates of unwanted issues to wrestle with: trust in God, life and death, grace and eternity, my vulnerability, my lack of control. Figuring out how to face fears cultivated over many decades was coming to a head with what sounded like a simple question: Would we stop on our way home to visit my brother? Everyone—my brother, my sister, my husband—had left the decision of whether to stop up to me. I was overwhelmed.

Intellectually, I knew the idea of not stopping was ridiculous, but everything within me wanted to say no. I was steeply inclined toward self-protection and flight. Maybe I could just tell everyone we really needed to get back home. Only I would know how

> **But Jesus immediately said to them: "Take courage! It is I. Don't be afraid."**
>
> —MATTHEW 14:27 (NIV)

much of a lie that was. Only I would have to live with the guilt of being the jerk of a big sister who couldn't stop because she was too scared and couldn't talk to anyone about it.

The rain slackened as I drove, and looking for comfort, I turned on a Christian music station. The Casting Crowns song "Oh My Soul" came on, and its opening lines caught my attention immediately: *Oh, my soul, oh, how you worry, oh, how you're weary from fearing you lost control. This was the one thing you didn't see coming* . . .

My rambling thoughts snapped to attention, transfixed. I marveled at how the lyrics so perfectly fit my emotions right then as they sang of hiding away—of losing faith and not believing. And there it was. All at once I knew the real choice wasn't about whether to stop and see my brother. It was whether I was going to believe in the goodness and love of God.

As the song continued, I felt the Spirit of God speaking directly to me: *Oh, my soul, You are not alone. There's a place where fear has to face the God you know. One more day.* I latched on to the phrase "one more day." This was an invitation. I also sensed a promise. Could God be telling me through this lyric that if I would give Him one more day—a day to go and see my brother and engage all the fear and pain I was imagining—He would show me how to lay all of that down? In the space of a verse and a chorus, the thought crystalized: Going to see Daniel might be a path forward. It could be God offering me a lifeline from this crippling fear. Could I dare to hope?

By the time we got to Charleston, West Virginia, around 2 p.m., I still hadn't fully committed to stopping to see my brother in Tennessee. Our possible destination was now only three hours away. I wanted to believe God's invitation, but fear and doubt had me second-guessing instructions to get out on that limb.

Now, everyone in the car was awake and hungry, and I was wrung out. Trying to get us to a lunch stop, I got lost and took a couple of wrong turns in the rain. More than one driver blew a horn at me. An older man shouted and gestured rudely at me through his windshield.

Finally, I managed to get the van pulled into a Chick-fil-A parking lot. I was at a breaking point physically, emotionally, and spiritually. I told my family to order without me, and I bolted to the restroom where I sobbed and sobbed in a stall, finally so broken I could only cry out for God to help me. *There's no way I can face seeing my brother. I cannot even manage to navigate to lunch without old men yelling at me. I cannot do the normal things of daily life without falling apart in exhaustion. How can I face seeing my brother like this?* I cried and cried. I was out of plans and out of ideas.

The only thing I had left was the only thing that matters: a strength other than my own. As I sobbed, I heard again God's invitation: *One more day, Elizabeth. Stay with this one more day; I will make a way for you—a way to see Daniel, to experience healing, a way to lay down fear, anxiety, the need to control everything, all that nasty bag of tricks you've been carrying and trying to pretend isn't there for so long. I will show you how to lay this down by looking things you dread square in the face, and when you get your head out of the sand, you will see Me.*

Suddenly I knew what I had to do. I knew I had to agree to see my brother the next day. I knew I had to trust this God who kept calling me out onto limbs with Him. The bigger risk would be to refuse.

I dried my eyes and found my family waiting for me so we could place our order together. While waiting, they had been chatting with one of the restaurant employees. My husband turned to me and said brightly, "He's a homeschooling dad who does CC." My youngest son was wearing a T-shirt bearing the logo of Classical Conversations, a national Christian homeschooling organization we were a part of. The employee had started a conversation with my son when he saw the shirt. He asked me a few questions, and we discovered we had led some of the same programs. He gave me a high-five. Suddenly the world

> **So do not fear, for I am with you; do not be dismayed, for I am your God. I will strengthen you and help you; I will uphold you with my righteous right hand.**
>
> —ISAIAH 41:10 (NIV)

seemed a little less terrifying, and it became a little more obvious that I was never out of God's line of sight. A stranger in an unfamiliar place saw a connection to a fellow believer and spoke up. God flooded me with peace and joy. As we sat down to eat, He whispered to me: *I see you. I love you. I know exactly where you are and exactly what you need.*

The rain had finally stopped by the time we left the Chick-fil-A that day. The storms in my heart had settled too. As we drove on, I knew I would go see my brother the next day and that God would see me through.

He did just that. My visit with Daniel was not any of the horrible, overwhelming things I imagined. It was a normal day hanging out with my brother, who was optimistic about his health. I gave God that one more day, and He began right then to make a pathway to wholeness and healing from my place of fear. He hasn't stopped healing me since.

40 Minutes
Mary Vee

I am an adventure seeker, especially when the activity involves mountains. I haven't done anything too crazy, like bungee jumping off a cliff, but I've climbed—sometimes crawled—obscure trails, and I've driven up to mountain peaks on narrow switchback dirt roads without guardrails, knowing the view of a lifetime awaited. Sunny days feel all the more vibrant in the mountains.

The day I left an inspiring Christian writers' conference near Ashville, the plan was to drive straight home. But the Blue Ridge Parkway sign with her earthen brown shades invited me to take a 3-hour detour—and so I did.

Forty spectacular, mouth-gaping minutes up and down the winding chiseled roadway—windows open, aerating my car with newly blossomed, candy-pink rhododendron scents—landed me at the ultimate scenic pull-off. It was the highest point accessible by vehicles, and the view was spectacular. Beyond the valley, ripples of mountain peaks pointed to their Maker.

But what attracted my attention more was a full double rainbow glowing in the valley below me. *I have to get a photo before it disappears.* I slammed the car into park, shut off the engine, grabbed my phone, and rushed to the edge. Two vibrant rainbows, one tucked under the other, in full-spectrum neon shades! Picture perfect photos. A trail to the side led me down to a point jutting into the valley. I stood on the edge, mesmerized by God's promise made long ago. To the left, dark clouds crawled over the mountains, enhancing the spectrum of colors. There would be no photo editing of these beauties.

I was alone with God in a sea of peaks overlooking a rainbow. I sang songs I learned at the writers' conference. Spoke God's Word out loud. Thanked Him for this beautiful place.

Tiny drops of moisture rode the wind and kissed me. A few clung to my clothes. I would have liked to stay longer, but growing winds warned of an imminent storm. As I rushed up the narrow path, the rain began in earnest, making the trail more slippery by the minute. *Just a few more feet to the car. I'll be out of the rain soon.*

The storm intensified faster than I expected. I could feel the temperature dropping around me. Puddles pooled in the parking lot. Hopping inside and turning on the heat couldn't happen soon enough. I pulled the handle and was thrown off balance when it wouldn't open. I didn't understand. I yanked again, sure I hadn't locked the doors. There would have been no reason to—I hadn't seen any other vehicles in the area, and none had pulled in since I arrived. I yanked again and looked through the window. My keys were on the seat. My raincoat, sweater, and umbrella were on the passenger seat. I walked around the car, tugging desperately on every handle, even the trunk door. They. Were. All. Locked. "God," I said out loud. "I need your help. I don't know what to do."

I took out my phone, shivers shaking my hands, and realized the service number was in my wallet. On the front seat.

I looked at my phone. Only 4 percent power remained, and less than a half bar for reception. I called home, but static shrouded the fifteen driving hours separating us, and we couldn't understand each other.

I debated about calling emergency services. Keys locked in a car was hardly an emergency. It was reckless. There had to be another way.

Thunder rumbled overhead. Lightning winked from the sky. Sheets of rain whooshed like ocean waves on me.

Ashamed, I dialed 911 and told the dispatcher my situation, especially the freezing part. She connected me to the park's ranger service. The ranger who answered asked me to repeat the story. I had to shout to be heard over the raging storm. He was at his son's soccer game near Asheville. It would take 40 minutes to drive to my location even if he left right away. I felt worse. This dad had to give up his son's game because of me. "I'm so sorry," I said.

> "The LORD your God, He is the One who goes with you. He will not leave you or forsake you."
>
> —DEUTERONOMY 31:6 (NKJV)

"It's part of the job, ma'am." The call ended, leaving me two percent battery.

The countdown to snuggling in my dry, warm, heater-on-full-blast car began.

Back at the trail, a scraggly tree grew up around a boulder the height of a chair. Its twisted efforts to survive with roots wedged under the cold rock gave me at least scanty shelter while I asked God what to do. In mid-conversation with the

Almighty, water collecting on leaves weighed the branches until they dropped, dousing an already drenched me. I was so cold. My fighting spirit kicked in again. I sloshed through the water to the road, shielding my eyes from the spray. Not a headlight penetrated the storm. No one drove by. No fool would drive this road in fierce weather. I crossed the street to the rocky cliff, seeking an alcove to shelter. There was none. Frustration gave way to panic. I returned to my vehicle, pulled on the handles, pounded on the window, and shouted, "Open!"

"Are you locked out?"

I turned. A man stood behind me—much too close for comfort.

Shocked to see anyone, I asked, "Where did you come from?"

"The trails." He circled my vehicle, looked in the windows, and yanked on the door handles as if I hadn't thought to do it. He leaned close to the passenger side and looked through the glass. At my stuff. My personal belongings. "I have a car," he said.

This man frightened me. He shouldn't have looked at my things. He shouldn't have checked each door. *And* I had not seen another vehicle in the lot the entire time I'd been there. "I'm OK. A ranger is on his way."

"I'm parked on the other side of the lot." The man inched uncomfortably closer. "You can wait inside until the ranger arrives."

When I was little, my parents and teachers said *never go with strangers*. Since then, I'd heard stories of angels in disguise. People who happened to show up at an oddly needed time. But my senses didn't believe this man to be one. "That's all right. The ranger said to wait by my vehicle."

"Suit yourself. I could move mine closer to yours if you prefer."

"Th-thank you. I'll be fine." I could land in the hospital with pneumonia—my teeth clacked with cold, stammering even my thoughts—but I'd be alive.

He vanished into a veil of rain. Strong winds heaved their power at my vehicle and me. Water dripped into my eyes, nose, and mouth. My fingers stiffened—so cold—I barely held on to the door handle. I felt flummoxed. I could not tolerate thirty or however many more minutes the ranger needed, but the man's offer of shelter didn't feel like the right solution.

Perhaps I shouldn't have resigned, but I did. Head bent, shoulders curled, I pushed through the wind in the direction the man had walked, crossing the lot. To my surprise, under the brush, hidden—who knows why—was a silver car. The man closed the trunk and walked to the front door.

"E-excuse me?"

> **But when [Peter] saw that the wind was boisterous, he was afraid; and beginning to sink he cried out, saying, "Lord, save me!" And immediately Jesus stretched out His hand and caught him.**
>
> —MATTHEW 14:30–31 (NKJV)

He turned and faced me with the same look I didn't trust. "Change your mind?" Maybe it was his bushy eyebrows, his imposing demeanor. He climbed in the driver's side, picked up items from the passenger seat, and set them in the back, then opened the passenger door from the inside.

One last chance to change my mind. I really didn't want to sit there. A deep reverberating bass roll of thunder forced my decision.

Wrapped in His Protection | 73

"This is a rental," he said. "That's why I don't have tools to break into your vehicle." A rhododendron blossom lay on the console between us. He carried on a light conversation about flowers and bugs found on his hike. "I only have this 110 camera. I wish I had a digital one like your phone. It's really nice. Can I borrow it? Take a photo of a blossom with rain droplets on it?"

No way would I hand him my only source of communication. "My device is almost out of power. You wouldn't happen to have a charge cord, would you?"

"Sorry. I only have a flip phone. Never bothered to upgrade." He showed me several low-grade flower pictures in his gallery. "If I could take a photo with your phone, I could email it to myself."

Not possible, I told him. But he pressed the topic, unwilling to let it drop. "Tell you what," I said. "I'll take a picture and email it to you."

He opened his door. "The rain has slowed. Let's do it now."

I could at least do this for him; after all, he gave me shelter. My guard remained on high alert every step to the nearest bush. I taught him to focus on the lighting, the droplet on the flower, the background gently focused, and snapped the shot.

He reached for my device. "May I try?"

No. "It's cold." I walked back to the rental. "You could explore your photo interests with a travel camera. Buy a good one. I'll send the photo once I have internet and my phone is charged."

He wrote his email address on scrap paper and gave it to me. Crackles, snaps, thunder, and rain drumming on the roof stifled the conversation. He at least turned on the engine when the windows fogged but then put the car in reverse. I reached for the door handle. "What are you doing?"

"I'm turning us around, so we can watch for the ranger." The car rolled away from the rhododendrons and overlook, swiveled, then stopped. He slipped the gear into park.

A wall of rain blurred my view. I longed for a ranger in uniform driving an official park truck to arrive. Instead, wind rocked the man's rental during the remaining silent minutes, lasting what felt like hours.

Two headlights sliced through the fog. An olive-drab ranger vehicle emerged in the lot. I opened my door and sloshed through puddles. "Thank you! Thank you for coming to help me." I barely finished speaking when the man appeared by my side.

He set his hand on my shoulder and told the ranger how he'd helped. I inched away from him, but he didn't leave.

> And he stayed on the mountain forty days and forty nights.
>
> —EXODUS 24:18 (NIV)

"You can get in the truck, ma'am. Sir, you can leave."

He didn't move. "I'd like to stay until she is safe inside her vehicle."

I waded around to the passenger side and climbed up to the seat.

"Sir. I said you can leave." The ranger remained in his truck, focused on the man.

"But—"

"I said, you can leave, sir."

The man finally returned to his car and slowly pulled away.

The ranger rolled up his window. "You know better than to accept help from strangers, right?"

GOD'S GIFT OF SIGHT
— Lynne Hartke —

AFTER A STORM, while water droplets are still in the air, the place to look for a rainbow is opposite the sun. To capture the best view, you need to look toward an uncluttered, dark background, such as clouds, a rock formation, or a mountain. This is because a rainbow is not solid, so its colors are best viewed against something that appears more solid and substantial than the ordinary sky. Perhaps more awe-inspiring than a rainbow itself, however, is the wonderful symbol of its appearance—God's pledge to humanity and all creatures to never again send a global flood (Genesis 9).

The 2-year-old inside me answered with my head lowered. "Yes." I knew it was a dangerous choice. But I had been so cold.

"I don't have tools to open doors, ma'am, but I can call a local locksmith. He lives a piece north of here. He'll want cash."

There may have been a quarter or two in my wallet. "I have a debit card. It's, um, locked in my car."

"You can work out the payment with him."

He spoke with the locksmith on the phone and then reported, "It'll take him 40 minutes to get here. It'll be safer to wait in the truck, ma'am."

Why was I not surprised the locksmith needed 40 minutes and not 15 or an hour? Forty had become the theme song of this day. God had used this number, a powerful storm, and a rainbow to remind me of what He did for Noah while showing His goodness, protection, and mercy to me. I was grateful to wait the 40 minutes.

The locksmith opened my car door, ending the ordeal. I waved goodbye to the ranger who had protected me and climbed inside my vehicle, turning the heater on full. As agreed, I followed the locksmith down the mountain to a local Walmart, where I used my debit card to withdraw sufficient money to pay for his services. To my delight, he let me take his photo. This, along with the pictures of the double rainbow, became my souvenir, my memory of the day God protected me.

A Sudden Halt

Robin T. Jennings

When I opened my eyes, I was hanging upside down from my seat belt. The last thing I remembered was losing control of our van and flipping into a ditch. I looked over at my wife. "Are you OK?" She said yes, but the back seat where our children sat was unnaturally silent.

Getting the oil changed and filling the gas tank in my wife's van seemed like preparation enough before our family had headed out that day. Although an attendant mentioned my tires needed replacing, I felt sure I could get another ten thousand miles out of them.

Besides, we were excited to pack and make the 10-hour drive from our home in Kentucky to pick up our eldest son from a Wisconsin summer camp. This was in the days before cell phones, and the only communication we'd had with him were camp postcards.

Traffic on the interstate was moving at a good pace, and I pushed hard to get to the camp quickly, as I was anxious to see our son. Much to my frustration, a rainstorm began to flood the road, and traffic around us reduced speed. As we neared our destination in Wisconsin, we drove on an old two-lane highway that was so uneven puddles soon formed. At times, I passed slow-moving cars and trucks. My wife encouraged me to ease up, but I felt as though I were in a race, and nothing was going to get in my way—especially a little rain.

Then the unthinkable happened. When I pushed down on the accelerator, the van started sliding across the highway. I turned the steering wheel to correct our direction, but it was unresponsive. We kept sliding, and I felt a sense of total helplessness as the van hydroplaned out of control. All I could do was look ahead in terror as we skidded at high speed off the highway into a ditch.

My wife screamed "Hold on!" to the kids. I said nothing; my mind was spinning just like the van, but my heart cried out for God to save us.

An eerie gushing sound of wind and rain accompanied us as we went airborne. Then the van twisted in flight and crashed into the ditch with a horrible sound and wrenching impact.

> **Create in me a pure heart, O God, and renew a steadfast spirit within me.**
>
> —PSALM 51:10 (NIV)

After checking on my wife, I tried to open the driver's door, but to no avail—the van had landed on its side. My wife and I struggled to push her door open, but it was crumpled shut. I yelled back at the older boys to try the sliding passenger doors, but one son's arm was somehow pinned from the crash while the other boy was busy trying to help the baby out of the car seat.

From outside, I heard banging on the doors and loud voices. Suddenly the passenger door opened, and hands from outside lifted my wife from the van. I reached back, grabbed one boy, and lifted him to someone on the other side and then raised the baby, who was now wailing, to another stranger.

I yelled out the window, "I have one boy pinned down. He can't move his arm."

I planned to stay with him, but a face popped through the window and encouraged me to climb out so they could help my boy. I was disoriented and clueless. Following orders made sense. Once outside, I felt sick looking at my family sitting on the side of the road huddled together under blankets. The sight of the van lying in the ditch struck horror in me as I realized my son's arm was pinned somewhere *underneath* the van.

By this time, about a half-dozen men stood beside my van, preparing to lift the vehicle and push it upright. I held my breath for the longest count in my life. I had no idea what to expect of my son's injuries. Would his arm be mangled or horribly bleeding? Grisly thoughts tore at my heart.

Seconds later, the van sat upright, and I watched my son pull his arm through the window. Relief flooded through me as I saw that both of his arms were moving and nothing appeared broken. His first words to me were, "Sorry, Dad. I guess the window was open and my arm went out when we crashed."

"I'm the one who is sorry." Never had I felt so low in my life. How could I have put my family at risk like that?

One of the men who helped us said, "Man, you were sure lucky."

I looked at him and looked at my totaled van behind him. With thoughts of my family swirling through my mind, I said, "What do you mean 'lucky'?"

His answer made me shiver. "Seconds after you went into the ditch, two logging trucks sped by. If you'd spun around just a little bit later, they would have hit you. That could have been really bad."

Another guy standing nearby entered the conversation by saying, "And be glad it was raining." Of course, I was not exactly in the mood to hear that until he added, "Fifty feet in front of you is a concrete drainage channel. You were lucky you flipped into a soft, wet ditch. Trust me, this accident could have been a lot worse."

I thanked the Good Samaritans as they began to leave and police and EMTs arrived. With their help, we contacted my parents, who were staying at a cabin near the camp. They retrieved our son from camp and drove to meet us. All the pieces came together except for one.

I was the missing piece. Life was no longer the same.

Over the next several weeks, I understood that I was the wreck. I was the one who had been out of control. The accident was not about luck; it was about faith. While the van had been hydroplaning, the steering wheel turned. My hands had let go. Faith let the Lord take over and drive. With two logging trucks coming at us, it was no coincidence the van flipped into a soft, wet ditch. The Lord had intervened with a saving miracle, and by His grace, none of us were hurt. I had never doubted that the Lord saved us, but it took time for me to realize God wanted me to turn over control over to Him—not only of the steering wheel, but also of my whole life. The accident was a wake-up call. It could have been just a moment in time that was easily forgotten, but the miracle opened my soul by shaping my relationship with the Lord, and He gave me a new life and hope for tomorrow.

> **He refreshes my soul. He guides me along the right paths for his name's sake.**
>
> —PSALM 23:3 (NIV)

Our boys are grown now, with wives and children of their own. During one recent visit, I watched through our living-room window as they drove away. No surprise, I still check their tires before they go.

After they were out of sight, I sat down with my wife. In my chair is a needlepoint pillow she made shortly after the van flipped into the ditch. It bore the words that told our story: "Call to me, and I will answer you" (Jeremiah 33:3, NIV).

Closing my eyes, I thanked the Lord for bringing my life to a halt and answering the call.

Dry in the Rain
Christel Owoo

"Do you see that? The rain in the other lane?" I asked my husband. He responded with an affirmative "Hmmm," his eyes fixed on the chaotic rush-hour traffic ahead of us.

We were eagerly anticipating a business dinner in Accra, the conclusion of our brief trip to Ghana. But dark clouds loomed above the winding highway as we drove back to the hotel at twilight. I peered into the darkness outside our car and noticed the cars in the oncoming lanes had slowed. Heavy rain fell relentlessly on their side of the road, their windshield wipers working hard to clear their view. Meanwhile, our lane was free from rain—not even one drop had fallen on our car or our part of the freeway.

A bolt of lightning lit the road for a second, and I expected rain to fall soon in our lane as well. Minutes ticked away, but there was still no sign of rainfall on our side of the highway, not even a drizzle. *We must be driving at the outer limit of the thunderclouds, causing rain to be in one area only*, I speculated, searching for an explanation for the strange weather pattern. Looking again, I realized that the limits of the clouds couldn't be the reason, because the freeway continued to meander through the hilly landscape, and with each turn our car remained dry. With each passing minute, the lightning flashes intensified in frequency, but still, not even one raindrop fell on our car.

God wants to show us something, I thought. I had no clue what it was, but it initially gave me a sense of peace. Ten minutes later, a rush of thoughts and questions flooded my mind. *Why is our car still dry? Even if rain touched the car, we would still be dry inside. Is our car important to God? I don't understand.* I frowned, confused about the message He was trying to send us.

Not long after, at the end of the highway, we could see a big intersection at the bottom of the hill, the last one before the crossing in front of our hotel. "Too much traffic there!" my husband murmured, his voice filled with frustration. Abruptly, he slammed on the car brakes and yanked the steering wheel to the right. With squeaking brakes, our car veered into the exit lane, just missing a minivan. Visibly angry, my spouse maneuvered the car into the line of cars heading uphill. It meant taking the longer route to our hotel—something he absolutely detests.

A deafening thunderclap pierced the silence, and soft rain peppered our car's roof. Ten minutes later, in the now-gushing rain, we finally reached the hotel. The hillside detour had cost us valuable time, and we hurried into the restaurant for our business dinner.

Midway through the amicable banquet, the unsettling sound of screams echoed from the lobby. Waiters with stern expressions hurriedly ran back and forth, their trousers rolled up to knee height.

"Did you hear that? What's going on in the lobby?" one business partner asked.

"I'm not sure, but it sounds pretty intense," my husband replied.

"Look at the waiters—they seem worried. And why are their trousers rolled up?" the other business associate said.

"I don't know. Let's ask the chief steward," my husband concluded.

The steward told us that water was flooding inside the lobby, creating a chaotic scene.

The flooding was starting to enter the dining room as well, inching closer and closer to our seats. Not wanting to interrupt our meeting, and assuming that if there was a danger the staff would tell us, we tried to ignore it and continue our meal. Gradually, the water sneaked its way under the table, finally stopping just before it reached my spouse and me. We locked eyes. "We kept our feet dry," we whispered. We finished eating and then wrapped up the meeting quickly, bidding farewell to our business partners.

Curious about the way the water seemed to avoid us, we proceeded to our chalet at the hotel compound. At the inner court, hotel personnel waded through knee-deep water—they signaled us to take another route. From the hillside on our left, the accumulated rainfall rushed down. The rainwaters were transforming the compound into a wild, turbulent stream. A helpful waiter volunteered to accompany us, carefully pointing out safe paths to follow. We arrived at our cabin—thankfully high enough on the hillside to avoid the rushing floodwater.

> **For he will command his angels concerning you to guard you in all your ways; they will lift you up in their hands, so that you will not strike your foot against a stone.**
>
> —PSALM 91:11–12 (NIV)

The plush beds beckoned us to a restful night's sleep. We were concerned that water might seep through our ceiling, but there were no visible leaks anywhere, despite the heavy rain. We slept peacefully.

The next morning, a bright sunbeam slipping through a gap in the curtains woke us up. The only sound that filled the room was the constant hum of the air conditioning. The rain had stopped. Outside, everything appeared calm. Colorful birds chirped, while a soft breeze rustled the gardens in the compound. Our footsteps echoed through the now-dry inner courtyard as we headed toward the restaurant, eager to savor a delicious breakfast. While we were drinking a good cup of English breakfast tea, my husband received concerned WhatsApp messages from friends in the Netherlands. The only two Dutch people who knew we were in Ghana enquired about our safety, as they could not reach us. Puzzled, my husband called them to find out what this was all about. They described horrible news reports from Ghana. A disaster had occurred the night before. Heavy rainfall had triggered floods, creating complete chaos and drowning several people in various places in the city. Lightning strikes had caused a petrol station to explode, killing many in the blaze. Realizing the extent of the danger from the floods, we mourned and prayed

> The LORD will keep you from all harm—he will watch over your life; the LORD will watch over your coming and going both now and forevermore.
>
> —PSALM 121:7–8 (NIV)

for those who had died and lost so much. And we gave thanks to God that we were safe.

We left the restaurant, and as we headed back to the hotel we crossed a small bridge over a narrow trench that usually only held puddles of stagnant, muddy water. But now the trench was full to the brim with patches of its riverbed soil all over the bridge. Tree branches, trash, and other debris were scattered over the road. An abandoned SUV lay flipped in a ditch farther down the street along with a few smashed passenger cars at a road bend.

Everywhere we went, we saw deserted streets and uprooted palm trees. We pressed on in silence, stunned by the destruction and in awe of the incredible force of nature.

Later that day, we learned that the severe flooding had swept away several cars at the exact junction where my husband had taken an abrupt turn the previous night. We exchanged a glance filled with relief and gratitude, silently thanking God for guiding us away from danger.

> **When you pass through the waters, I will be with you; and when you pass through the rivers, they will not sweep over you.**
>
> —ISAIAH 43:2 (NIV)

We now also understood the reason that our car had been kept dry on the drive into the city. God's intention was not merely to shield us from the rain, but to remind us of His presence. He kept our car dry, against all odds, because He wanted us to be fully aware of the rare circumstances that were taking place and to give Him all the glory for a miracle.

We returned to the Netherlands the following day and resumed our normal lives, like the Israelites who forgot about God's mighty deliverance through the Red Sea. It wasn't until 3 weeks later that we truly grasped the dry-in-the-rain-miracle and saving work of our God.

After a church service, one of our fellow congregants approached us, sipping on a steaming cup of coffee. He had been looking for us and eagerly asked about our well-being. "Recently, on a Tuesday evening at the start of my prayer meeting, I suddenly felt a deep urge to pray for the two of you," he shared. "I persuaded my family members to join me in fervent prayer. We ended up interceding for you the entire evening. Anyway, I don't know the exact date, but that same week, my sister called me from Ghana and told me about the flooding disaster."

My husband and I realized that our friend's urge to pray for us happened on the exact day and time we were in our car on the way back to the hotel.

"We were in Ghana at that time!" we shouted simultaneously and told him about the dry car.

God had orchestrated our deliverance—from our dry car; to prompting my husband to take an abrupt turn; to our friend, over 3,000 miles away, pushing his covenant family to intercede for us all evening. It was all part of God's plan. God had touched people's hearts to cover us with prayer when they were unaware of our whereabouts and the surrounding dangers.

Guilt washed over me, as I realized I had taken God's blessings for granted. I hadn't fully grasped the magnitude of His rescue—the profound impact of God's intervention and His desire for us to recognize His saving grace. But now I realized the power of prayer, the importance of gratitude, and God's hand in even the smallest details.

On the Road with God
Sandra Ardoin

The cold December evening surrounded me as I slid behind the wheel of my husband's 23-year-old, well-loved compact car. I drew in a deep breath and took one last glance at the house.

This is it.

With a last turn of the key, we locked the front door of our home—now someone else's—ready to put our life in Texas in the rearview mirror.

I pressed the clutch and shifted into gear, glad to know my husband followed in the pickup truck, towing a U-Haul trailer. Even under the best of circumstances, driving a vehicle with a manual transmission sapped my confidence. Now, I'd need to rely on what I learned from my husband about driving a stick shift to guide his little car over 1,200 miles. And did I mention that I'd be pulling a trailer with a small boat on a busy city highway in rush-hour traffic? No pressure!

After many discussions about the attraction of North Carolina and its closer proximity to family, we began to pray about a move east. We saw ourselves living among the rolling hills. A landscape cool and green. A Carolina blue sky. Trees so tall it was a strain on the neck to see their tops.

God had answered our prayers that summer when my husband announced his company's approval for him to work out of their Charlotte office. The confirmation of God's blessing came when my husband said, "They've offered to pay for a mover." Wow! My heart danced at the realization that what we had envisioned would soon be a reality.

Now I steered away from the curb, hoping the car's heater would kick in soon and warm the interior, along with my nose and hands. Only days before Christmas, and the Dallas meteorologists called for cold rain and ice.

If only we had gotten an earlier start in order to beat the bad weather, but that morning's house closing hadn't gone as smoothly as we'd planned, and the movers were hours late. As a result, we faced a night-long, non-stop drive to Mobile, where we planned to celebrate Christmas with my in-laws before settling in a new home. I cringed at the prospect of 24 hours without sleep.

I said goodbye to the close-set houses of the neighborhood, their colorful Christmas lights twinkling like the stars that were hidden by winter storm clouds. Bundled in the front seat of the truck, alongside my husband, sat our 4-year-old daughter with our dog on the floorboard at her feet. Our vehicles together must have looked like a skimpy wagon train on the move.

I drove past familiar places for the last time, ready to but nervous about settling into an area I'd only visited twice. In that moment, I understood the temptation Lot's wife faced—the desire to look back, to change my mind. But I drove on.

Our small town had grown larger with each new subdivision. The entire area had outgrown us. We longed for that small-town feel—the uncrowded roadways, the "Howdy, neighbor" wave. I missed things like the simplicity of a library housed in a decades-old residential bungalow. Our area of North Texas was no longer sprawling prairie land, but a finger in the hand of a sprawling metroplex.

I headed east on I-20, watching the traffic and the sky, fearing the rain that could make the journey treacherous. Even though my husband followed close behind, it was lonely inside the dark vehicle with no one to talk to. At least he had our daughter for however long she stayed awake. My company was the memory of months of preparation and planning, the effort to sell the house and pack. It had all culminated in today's whirlwind of activity and stress.

Not far outside Dallas, I glanced at the dashboard gauges and gasped. Oh boy. I had enough car sense to know what I saw from the oil pressure gauge wasn't good, and I couldn't drive far with that gauge taunting me. Spotting a truck stop, I took the exit off the interstate and pulled into a corner of the parking lot, my eye on the rearview mirror to be sure my husband noticed and followed.

> **By day the LORD went ahead of them in a pillar of cloud to guide them on their way and by night in a pillar of fire to give them light, so that they could travel by day or night.**
>
> —EXODUS 13:21 (NIV)

He pulled alongside me and got out. "What's the matter?"

"The oil pressure dropped to zero."

Being a car guy who knew his little vehicle inside and out, he raised the hood and soon found that the seals on the valve cover gasket had blown. Oil had leaked onto the manifold—the whole engine, really—creating a smoke cloud.

He shuffled through the items in the trunk, shut the lid, and gave God praise that the tools he needed to get us back on the road were in the trunk and not the moving van. A few minutes later, he came out of the convenience store relieved and proclaiming it a miracle that they had the heavy viscosity of oil required to seal the valves.

With a long way to go, we weren't out of the woods. Would the little car bear up? Thankfully, after only encountering a few raindrops on the windshield, we outran the threat of bad weather.

I hit Shreveport, still trailing a cloud of smoke like a torpedoed ship. Swirling lights in the rearview mirror caught my attention. I checked my speed. Not a problem under the circumstances. Still, the police followed me onto the shoulder of the interstate.

Great. I'm about to get a ticket for polluting the Louisiana landscape.

As the two officers approached my car, my husband parked behind them and opened his door. He had a foot on the pavement when an officer issued a command. "Stay inside the vehicle, sir."

As my husband watched, helpless to do anything, they checked my license and listened to my story about our move and the oil still burning on the manifold. I breathed a sigh of relief when I eased back on the road a few minutes later—without a ticket.

On overnight drives, I love seeing the sun rise over the horizon. In a matter of minutes, it turns the sky from deep

> You make your saving help my shield, and your right hand sustains me; your help has made me great.
>
> —PSALM 18:35 (NIV)

indigo colors to the shades of a ripening peach to lighter blues—the satisfying start of a new day.

Not that morning.

I had been up for more than 20 tense hours with several hours of driving to go before we reached Mobile. I was tired and hungry and knew my husband and daughter must be too. One thing kept us going. We were close to rest—so close.

We stopped for a quick breakfast along US 49 in Mississippi before reaching Interstate 10. Amid some road construction, I turned off the highway and into a fast-food restaurant parking lot. Being a boat trailer-pulling rookie, parking in the small lot was challenging.

Forward. Reverse. Angle. Turn right, turn left. Jackknife.

I looked over my shoulder. The men working on the road had stopped their progress to watch mine—and laugh. Fortunately, my husband came to my rescue. *Just bring my food to the car. I'll be waiting under the front seat.*

> "I have told you these things, so that in me you may have peace. In this world you will have trouble. But take heart! I have overcome the world."
>
> —JOHN 16:33 (NIV)

After breakfast, I turned the key in the ignition, worried the car wouldn't start. I worried for no reason. Pulling back on the road, I gladly left behind the amused construction workers. Hours later than expected, we crept down my in-laws' driveway. We spent our next hours resting, but it was the end of the line for our poor, sickly vehicle. When we left Mobile, we borrowed my father-in-law's pickup to pull the boat the rest of the way to our new home.

I would like to say that my thoughts, mile after mile, centered on thanksgiving with each blessing we had received over that period of 24 hours. I can't. I was too caught up in the moment's anxiety to appreciate God's provision and protection.

Even though I would have preferred a smooth trip, time has allowed me to look in the rearview mirror and see His hand over us during every hour. He provided the dry weather, the right viscosity of oil, the proper tools, and two understanding police officers. He kept us from being stranded and vulnerable on the side of the road in the middle of the night. He gave that little car just enough *oomph* to get us to family.

The experience has been an enduring reminder that God never promised me a life free from potholes and hazards, but He did promise to remain at my side along the journey. I believe wholeheartedly that I can rest in the peace and security of His presence, even when, sometimes, it still takes seeing my troubles from a little distance to appreciate God's faithfulness.

God Is in the Details
Tina Wanamaker

What was I thinking?

I sat there in the airport waiting to board my flight. I was heading to Kenya—alone. I thought about a woman I knew who had traveled to New Guinea by herself. She said she was either incredibly obedient to God or flat crazy. Perhaps you need to be both to do something like that. I was about to find out as I stepped out into this adventure with Jesus.

The idea of traveling to Kenya had come to me the year before. My friend Sister Elizabeth, who lived there, had been inviting me to come and teach at a Bible conference for a few years. Each year I told her no, but not this year. Something was different. I had an understanding that I should go. I might have dismissed this understanding, except that at the same time the Lord had provided the funding for the trip. A sister in Christ had given me some money. As she handed it to me, she told me it was for ministry. Even as I opened that envelope, I knew it was for Kenya.

And so here I was, ready to board the first leg of my flight—heading into the unknown. Feeling a little crazy. Or obedient. I wasn't sure. Little did I know how I would see God show up.

The first flight of my journey ended up arriving an hour behind schedule. I got off the plane in Seattle and ran through the airport, pushing my luggage in front of me. Out of breath,

I arrived at the gate for my connecting flight to Dallas—which, the young man at the counter informed me, I had just missed. He was able to re-route me, but now I would have a 3-hour wait there in the airport. I'd also have an 8-hour layover in Dallas. Due to the re-routing, I would be unable to make my connecting flight and would have to wait for the international flight the next day.

I walked slowly away from the counter, silently praying, *Lord, I know You must have a purpose in this. Please use this.* I was going to miss my first few meetings in Kenya due to the late arrival, but I remembered that prior to the trip I had prayed that God would have the fullness of His way in every detail of my journey. With this in mind, I chose not to worry about it and instead to look for God's purpose. I found my next gate and went to get something to eat. When I returned, there was a man in his twenties sitting nearby. I began a conversation with him and soon we were discussing his life. He shared that his name was Allen and he was a former drug user. He had gotten clean when he had a child 2 years before.

As we continued to talk, I asked questions and listened to his answers. He was interested in hearing about the Lord. I had been shopping at a thrift store a few weeks before and the woman at the counter gave me a Bible. I told her I'd take it on my trip with me and give it away as the Lord led. This was the

> **And we know that all things work together for good to those who love God, to those who are the called according to His purpose.**
>
> —ROMANS 8:28 (NKJV)

leading. Allen received the Bible, and I left him with it opened on his lap.

God had a purpose for the interruption of my schedule. I had asked the Lord to arrange each step of that trip, as He had already done, even before I'd left the United States. I had more conversations as I waited, but the highlight of that layover was talking with the young man.

From Seattle, I boarded the flight to Dallas. Once there, I did my best to curl up on the seats during my wait and get a little sleep while I waited for my flight to the Middle East. During that time, the reality that I was about to travel very far from home suddenly hit me, and I asked the Lord to send me a friendly face.

Not long after my prayer, we began to board the plane. I found my seat at the back, and soon a man sat down next to me. He settled into his seat and greeted me with a smile. We began to chat, and I learned he was an American serviceman flying to his next assignment. He had been married for just about the same number of years as my husband and I, and he had children around the same ages as ours. And He loved the Lord. God had sent a friendly face!

> **Trust in the LORD with all your heart, and lean not on your own understanding; in all your ways acknowledge Him, and He shall direct your paths.**
>
> —PROVERBS 3:5–6 (NKJV)

This man ended up being an incredible blessing to me on many levels. We talked about the Lord and our families. He gave me travel tips. We prayed together at the end of the flight. He got my luggage down from the overhead bin, then he introduced me to other servicemen when we disembarked, and they helped me find the gate for my next flight.

Finally, I was on my last flight, this one to Nairobi. This flight went without any issues. I sat next to a young woman and had a wonderful conversation. We landed and exited the plane around 11:30 p.m.

At the time, there were still Covid restrictions in place, which meant extra checkpoints. I waited in a long line and finally made it to the front. The agent looked at my paperwork and said, "No, you can't come in with this." He told me to step aside, which I did while he helped the next person in line. I stood there confused and sent up a prayer for help. The thought occurred to me that maybe a different document would work. I pulled out another piece of paper and got back in line. I passed him this next paper. He took his time looking it over and then told me a word I was hoping to hear: "Go." I went!

> "Call upon Me in the day of trouble; I will deliver you, and you shall glorify Me."
>
> —PSALM 50:15 (NKJV)

The next stop was to get my visa checked before I could have my luggage processed. The lines seemed incredibly long for this step. I took my place at the end of the correct line and waited and waited. By this time, I wasn't feeling all that well because I'd had so little sleep over the past few days. An airport worker came by and looked me over. She asked, "Are you sick?" My response garnered a smile from her: "No, I'm not sick. I just haven't slept in a few days, and I know I look terrible!" She walked on.

Finally, I arrived at the desk. I somehow was the last one in line. It was around 1:30 a.m. by that point. I passed my visa and passport to the woman. She looked at the passport and then the visa. Not looking up, she said, "You've got the wrong kind of visa."

It took a moment for that statement to register in my brain. "What do you mean?"

She explained that I had gotten a children's visa instead of an adult visa. Although the information was all correct, it was the wrong kind. She couldn't let me in because of that. She informed me that I could apply for the right kind at 9 a.m. when the counter opened in the morning.

I looked around me and wondered what to do. I imagined myself curled up outside the building waiting for morning to come and the visa counter to open. I had no options. I just stood there looking at her. At that moment the woman who had approached me earlier and asked if I was sick arrived at the counter. She leaned over and said to the lady, "This lady missed a flight and hasn't slept in some time. Is there anything we can do?" The visa woman looked at me and asked why I was in Kenya. I told her I was there to teach at a Bible conference.

She looked down and began writing something in my passport. "Do you have $51?" I said yes. I gave it to her, and she handed me back my passport and told me she had written down a visa number for me and to use that while in the country. I nodded, not understanding. Then she said, "You can go." I realized that she was letting me through, and I went quickly before she could change her mind. At last I was able to get through the final baggage check and meet my contacts outside.

The flights to Kenya were just the beginning. The Lord continued to lead for the rest of the trip in incredible ways. He truly was in the details. I saw this clearly: God has a plan and brings things together for the good in seemingly miraculous ways. By the time I was ready to leave Kenya, I knew for certain that there is nothing flat crazy about being obedient to God.

Look for the helpers. You
will always find people
who are helping.

—Fred Rogers

CHAPTER 3

God Sends His Helpers

Totally Lost, but Not Alone 104
    Betty A. Rodgers-Kulich
God Knew I Needed Help 110
    Mindy Baker
The Fourth of July Miracle 115
    Carolyn Waverly
A New Definition of Snow Angels 121
    Cynthia A. Lovely
Mini Miracles on the Cancer Journey 126
    Stephanie A. Wilsey
God's Gracious Gifts 133
    Wendy Lynne Smith
Walking in Faith and Prayer 140
    Stacy Leicht
God Is Always on Call 145
    Elizabeth Erlandson

Totally Lost, But Not Alone

Betty A. Rodgers-Kulich

Who would think that a short leisurely hike at Arches National Park would turn life-threatening? Certainly not on that beautiful sunny day, when my husband and I had no clue what awaited us.

We are inexperienced hikers; walking the flat bike trails at a local city park was our only real experience, and we were not savvy about the rigors involved in a serious hike or the need for specialized clothing, equipment, water, and energy bars. So, after viewing maps of various hikes at the park's welcome center, we chose the shortest loop that would show us a couple of the famed arches up close. After that, we decided we would just see the views from our rental car as we drove to various park lookout points. We set out in shorts and tennis shoes with ankle-high socks, armed with Twizzlers, a two-liter bottle of water, and a simple map of various trails and sights.

The arches stretched over a large, wide gulch with a flat dry riverbed. Excited to see the first arch, we stopped and took some pictures, discussed the various rock formations and how water must have eroded the arches. The 15-minute hike hadn't been strenuous, so we studied the rudimentary map, located the rock markers, and continued on to the second arch. As we walked in this next section, we noticed that there was a slight incline in the riverbed and the walls of the gorge were changing. On we traveled, caught up in the austere beauty of the area, enraptured by the colors of the stone walls, boulders, and riverbed rocks. About another 15 to 20 minutes later, we realized we had not seen the second arch. Stopping under a small tree growing out of the side of the gorge to look at the map, we concluded we had to be close and pressed on. We came to another arch, but our arrival confirmed the shape of the arch didn't resemble the sketches on the map. We shared the water, taking it down to half a bottle, then opened the Twizzlers and consumed the entire package.

Looking at the time, our trek had now taken twice as long as the map suggested it would. But we weren't worried because we had taken our time and enjoyed the sights. According to the map, the loop circled back to the visitor center just up ahead. Onward we hiked.

> **For it is written, He will give His angels charge over you to guard and watch over you closely and carefully; and on their hands they will bear you up, lest you strike your foot against a stone.**
>
> —LUKE 4:10–11 (AMPC)

The short morning hike was turning into something we hadn't expected. Could we be lost? Certainly not! We had followed every rock cairn formation, and hadn't we seen the first arch that matched the map's drawing? The return loop must be ahead. We thought about turning around and going back the way we had come and started to backtrack. But we soon realized that everything looked different and more confusing to follow. Taking a few sips of the low drinking water supply, we turned and forged ahead, trying to stay in the shadows of the now-taller gorge walls. Surely the center was just ahead.

Onward we walked, exhausted, hungry and now more concerned about our well-being as the sun had reached its zenith and was now slowly heading in the other direction. We concluded that our inexperience had led us up a never-ending arroyo. We were lost. Now what?

Our water was gone, we had no food, and—since this was before cell phones—no way to let someone know what happened. We were in a precarious situation. I wanted to cry from the fatigue and uncertainty. Should we turn around or keep going? We stopped in the shade of a large boulder that sat at the side of the now-narrow gorge. The walls had gradually become considerably higher and were no longer scalable. The floor of the riverbed had lots of scrub brush and trees. In the far distance was another arch that had a very unusual and unique shape.

Worries about dehydration or an encounter with a mountain lion or a rattlesnake in the now-dense foliage and undergrowth were running through our minds. My husband prayed, "God, what do we do?" I prayed too, for wisdom and a miracle.

After praying for several minutes, I pulled out the map and just stared at it. What had happened? How had we gotten to this point? Had we missed some rock cairn markers? Had someone or something moved them, causing us to take a wrong path? *God, how do we escape?*

I had a strong feeling that I should take another look at the map. It didn't make sense to me when we'd already spent so much time staring at it, but I took another look. Then I saw it. The oddly shaped arch we'd seen in the distance was on the map, but it was almost at the other end of the park, not near the visitor center. It was on a trail for "experienced hikers." Could we really have become that lost and traveled that far? The setting sun verified how long we had been hiking. I showed the map to my husband and said, "I think this is where we are."

He studied the map and confirmed his agreement. The map showed an exit egress right before the unique arch at the last overlook for the park scenic road—the very one we had planned to drive to. Certainly, we could find the exit. But there was a distance yet to cover and the sun was almost hidden behind the wall of the arroyo. The shadows began to take shape around us.

We trudged on with spent limbs and labored steps, trusting in God's protection and deliverance. As we rounded a bend, we spooked a giant buck that leaped out, nearly running us over. The fright took our last reserves of adrenaline. Dehydrated, sunburned, and exhausted, we came to the area marked on the map for the way out to the parking overlook and scanned the sheer walls for a sign directing us out. But all we saw were metal rebar rungs ascending the sheer, 40-foot arroyo wall. I wanted to scream and cry at the same time. I looked up but only saw the guardrail marking the parking for the overlook. No one was standing admiring the arch. In fact, as the sun was dipping below our horizon, the silence was deafening. We looked at each other and hung our heads. Tears were absent in our dehydrated state. Praying for strength, we asked for God's mercy to help us make the climb out.

> **Oh, taste and see that the LORD is good; blessed is the man who trusts in Him!**
>
> —PSALM 34:8 (NKJV)

With a rubbery arm I reached out and touched the rebar only to find it hot from the day's sun. How would we do this? Looking up at this angle, the height seemed impossible even on a good day, but our lives depended on successfully making that climb. My husband wanted me to go first. I knew why. He thought he could catch me if I slipped. I prayed, "God, help us take one rung at a time and not think about the impossibility of doing this. Help us to focus on Your promise to work all things for our good."

Taking what seemed like an hour, we climbed out to an empty parking lot and collapsed against the guard rail for support as the last rays of the sun started dipping below the horizon. The air felt cold against our sunburned bodies, and we were miles from the visitor center.

> **No harm overtakes the righteous.**
>
> —PROVERBS 12:21 (NIV)

I prayed, "God, help us again! Thank You for getting us up that wall, but we need more help. Give us moonlight to see and strength to walk. You got us this far; please continue to help us."

Stepping out onto the road, we heard a vehicle coming toward us. Would it be the park ranger looking for us because we had not signed out of the guest book? The headlights prevented us from seeing who it was at first. It was a rusted-out pickup truck, not a park ranger, and the driver's scruffy appearance made me nervous.

He pulled over to us and asked why we were out here without a vehicle. My husband stepped up to the window and explained our plight.

"You could have died out there! That area floods in an instant. If it had rained up country, the flood waters would have swept you away, not to mention rattlesnakes and mountain lions. Besides, the temperatures are even higher down on the riverbed from the reflection off the rock walls. How much water did you have with you?" We told him and he shook his head. "Hop in, and I'll take you back to the welcome center. You'd never make it on foot."

Was this man God's provision for us or an unsavory character who couldn't be trusted? We had asked for His help. We had to trust that God had spared our lives this far and He wasn't going to let them end now.

That trust turned out to be justified; the stranger drove us back to the safety of the welcome center and our car. As I watched our rescuer drive away, I wondered how God had gotten him here in just the right time to see us and help us get back. It really didn't matter. God had chosen him to be our angel—guiding him to the right spot just as He had watched over us throughout the day.

God Knew I Needed Help

Mindy Baker

Last summer I fell and broke my ankle during a family vacation to Arizona. One minute I was surrounded by a gorgeous canyon, navigating a rocky streambed, simply enjoying the wonder of God's beautiful creation. The next minute I was in an ambulance being rushed to the hospital after an emergency rescue team carried me out on a stretcher. Life can change in an instant.

After surgery to repair the ankle, I received the devastating prognosis. I could not bear weight on the injured ankle for 6 weeks. As I tried to process the news, I began to mentally review my schedule over the coming weeks, and the reality of what these limitations would mean slowly sank in. Panic bubbled up inside me.

I am a teacher, and my inability to be on my feet without assistance meant that I would have to miss several weeks of school, and I not be able to start the year with my classes. My mind reeled as I thought about all of the preparations that I would need to put into place in order for my classroom to get off to a good start without me.

While I was still thinking about the school situation, my husband reminded me of an even bigger issue that I hadn't remembered: He was going on a three-week work trip to India.

It was a trip that required his presence, and changing the dates was not an option. He would not be at home to help me for several weeks of my recovery.

As we finished our conversation with the doctor, I remained calm on the outside, but on the inside my heart pounded like a galloping horse, and my mind swirled with worry. I tried to convince myself that I would be fine alone during the weeks of my husband's trip, but I was afraid. On the way home, I prayed, "Lord, help my ankle to heal quickly!" That was not the prayer that God chose to answer. There would be nothing quick about my healing process.

We have a two-story house with our bedroom on the second floor. Because climbing the stairs was not possible, we purchased a bed for me to set up camp downstairs. Elevating my leg, taking Tylenol, and sipping frozen lemonades is what I remember most about the first few days home.

> "Your Father knows what you need before you ask him."
>
> —MATTHEW 6:8 (NIV)

Navigating from the bed to the couch to the bathroom and occasionally outside to the back patio was the extent of my daily routine. Dry shampoo became my best friend. I also remember the day that Amazon delivered a helpful basket to tie onto the front of my walker. Being able to put a book or a travel mug of coffee into the basket of my walker while maneuvering to the couch by myself was invigorating. But deep down, I felt very dependent on others and hated it. And my husband was scheduled to leave in a week. *What am I going to do?*

My husband had the same question. "You're going to need some help," he said. "Who do you want to ask?"

I thought about how to answer his question. As empty nesters, my kids were not able to help me to the extent I needed. My extended family lived hours away. Friends were already bringing meals, and I didn't want to be a burden. The true answer was that I didn't want to ask anyone. I was too stubborn. And proud.

"I'll be fine," I told him, trying to act very confident. "I can do it." That probably sounded comical given the amount of nothing that I was able to do on my own at that time. In a moment alone with the Lord, I prayed, "Lord, you know I need help. What should I do? I feel discouraged and alone."

> "Look at the birds of the air; they do not sow or reap or store away in barns, and yet your heavenly Father feeds them. Are you not much more valuable than they?"
>
> —MATTHEW 6:26 (NIV)

A day later, God's mercy and provision took my breath away. I received an astonishing call from my friend Donna, who lived on the East Coast—hundreds of miles from my home in Indiana. Diana knew about my accident and my husband's trip. "My schedule is free for the next few weeks, and I feel that God has told me to come and help you. What do you think?"

I didn't know what to say. I was speechless. I wanted to deny that I needed help, but the reality screamed otherwise. God had provided exactly what I needed in the exact moment that I needed it. My friend, prompted by God, was offering to help me. I didn't have to ask. I wouldn't have even thought to ask. But now all I had to do was say yes.

GOD'S GIFT OF SIGHT
— Kim Taylor Henry —

GOD'S MANY NAMES reflect His attributes. One of God's names is El Roi, which means "The God who sees me." It proclaims that wherever a person is, no matter what they say or do, however they feel, whatever emotions they experience, God sees and knows it all. He is aware of every circumstance, word, action, and thought in everyone's life. His sight encompasses the external and the internal. Yet He loves fully and completely in spite of the flaws and failings that we all have. That is the true miracle of El Roi.

"If you are sure you want to, that would be great," I said in a wobbly voice.

"I'm sure," she said. "It will be fun, you'll see."

A few days later my husband went to India, and Donna came to stay with me. To my amazement, not only did God nudge Donna to come and help me, but He also provided a donor to pay for her flight to my city. And then He provided different friends who were willing to give her rides to and from the airport. The blessings kept stacking up.

While she was here, we had an amazing time. We watched movies, played board games, and even put together a very complicated puzzle. We often sat out on the back patio, sometimes laughing together and at times praying together. She helped me with needed tasks around my house. She was there when I made the transition from using a walker to a scooter, and she also helped me start back to school successfully, both logistically and emotionally.

But most of all, because she was there, I wasn't alone. Her presence was a huge comfort. She showed me not only the beauty and blessing of serving others, but also the importance of saying yes to God when He prompts you to do something. Because she said yes, I was the recipient of God's blessing. The entire experience was humbling, because it has never been easy for me to admit I need help. But God has used this experience to show me His sovereign power and the beautiful way that He knows my needs, provides for my needs, and wraps me in His protection.

> And my God will meet all your needs according to the riches of his glory in Christ Jesus.
>
> —PHILIPPIANS 4:19 (NIV)

The Fourth of July Miracle
Carolyn Waverly

As I reached for the gallon of milk from the grocery's dairy case, my cell phone rang. It was 9 p.m. With my 96-year-old mother in a full-care facility, I expected it to be a call from Mom's nurse.

"Are you Elizabeth's mother?"

It was a police officer. I answered yes, my heart racing as I heard him speaking to someone, asking questions. The person responded, and I recognized my daughter's voice, pitiful and lost. More fragile than my elderly mother, our daughter Elizabeth, an alcoholic, was teetering on a precipice. Alone. Intoxicated. Helpless. Far away on a Chicago street. With swarms of people. On the Fourth of July.

I thought back to a month before Easter when I was walking out of church, and a friend had asked about Elizabeth. As I shared a bit of our latest saga, my friend nodded. Her son was 5 years sober, and she knew the difficulties we faced all too well. "I once prayed for an Easter miracle. God answered that prayer." She spoke with boldness. "I'm going to pray that prayer for Elizabeth!"

When I got home, I wrote in my journal, "I am praying for an Easter miracle!" I prayed each and every day. But when my husband, Will, picked Elizabeth up from the train station the night before Easter, she clearly had been drinking. Not exactly the miracle I'd prayed for so diligently.

Elizabeth's roommate would text or call with stories of Elizabeth's dangerous behavior. I could barely get my mind around what she said Elizabeth was doing. Her roommate moved out before their lease ended, leaving me with no way to contact Elizabeth if she didn't answer her phone. For my April 29 journal entry, I wrote, "One crisis passes only to be replaced by another. Grant us grace, more grace, God. Send someone kind and helpful if Elizabeth needs aid or assistance, Lord! Protect her. I beg you, Lord Jesus, to keep Your mighty hand and outstretched arms around her. This is taking such a toll on Will and me. We *never* would have guessed we'd have to go through this fire. Calm my mother's heart!"

> Wait for the LORD; be strong and take heart and wait for the LORD.
>
> —PSALM 27:14 (NIV)

Elizabeth, our firstborn, was innately driven to excellence, to the point of perfection. By middle school, we sought a counselor to help her—and us—through anorexia and to identify and treat her obsessive and compulsive behaviors. She was such a kind, compassionate, and caring teenager with good friends. She won academic honors, and when she went away to college, she chose a double major, tutored on the side, and still made the dean's list. She worked hard. Too hard. When setbacks came, whether it was a breakup or a job being eliminated, she found it nearly impossible to let it go.

After Elizabeth had a panic attack that resulted in her totaling her car, she reluctantly went to an appointment I made with a psychiatrist at our church. I talked to professionals, sought a counselor for personal guidance in how to respond, and rallied my little trio of praying friends. But with her living alone and far away, there were limits to what Will and I could do. We didn't even know if she was taking her medication.

Elizabeth found her own way to cope. Binge drinking eventually shifted to out-of-control addiction. A call from a police officer or ER doctor would jolt us out of bed in the late hours of the night.

After one of those unnerving phone calls, I located an Al-Anon meeting nearby. We learned about alcoholism as a disease, and how we had prolonged her addiction by enabling. Instead of trying to force her to do what we thought was best, we started asking, "What is your plan?"

Eventually, she saw the Christian counselor we offered to pay for. She went to AA meetings. I researched treatment centers, and we tried to discuss them with her. She refused. "I'm NOT going to rehab!"

> **God is within her, she will not fall; God will help her at break of day.**
>
> —PSALM 46:5 (NIV)

That Fourth of July night, just as we got home from the grocery store, the policeman called again. "Please do not put her on the train to her apartment! Even if she insists! I will pay for an Uber," I pleaded. "Does she have the key to her apartment?"

"Let me check . . . yes, she does. I see it," he responded. "What's her address? I have to go, ma'am. I'll call you back."

Will and I knelt by our fireplace. We couldn't control our daughter's behavior when she lived across town after college. We certainly couldn't control her actions 3 hours away on a packed street in Chicago. Would Elizabeth understand her whereabouts enough to let herself into the massive apartment building, use two separate keys, and walk up two flights of stairs? I called one of her friends. Voice mail. I tried to contact her AA sponsor via Facebook. Nothing.

On my knees, I cried out to God, *Rescue her!* I had prayed Psalm 91 for her protection so many times that I knew many of the lines from memory. *Rescuer. Protector. Deliverer.*

The answer came in the midst of my prayer. Janet! I jumped up from my knees. My best friend. Several days before, Janet had casually mentioned she'd be visiting her daughter and family in the Chicago suburbs over the holiday. *Would I be asking too much? Even for a best friend?* I dreaded making that call, but I didn't have any other ideas.

"What are you doing?" I asked Janet when she answered the phone.

"Just reading a story to my grandgirl. In my jammies." Then she added, "What's up?" She knew me well.

"I have the biggest favor I've ever asked you. Would you drive to Elizabeth's building to see that she gets into her apartment safely?" I asked.

"Yes. Text me her address." She didn't hesitate or even ask questions.

Eventually, the policeman called to say Elizabeth had left in a Lyft. Because Janet was staying in the suburbs, she wouldn't get there first. If Elizabeth arrived before her and was able to get into the apartment building, Janet wouldn't even know. I had neither control nor power. *Only my Father Above does.* I stayed on my knees.

The wait was excruciating, the list of what-ifs so long! Finally, Janet called. She spoke those three sacred words: "I see her!"

The next moments were a blur of words and emotion. "Oh honey!" I heard my friend say to Elizabeth, like a mother bird swooping from the sky to rescue one of her own just in the nick of time. "You're safe." I could hear Elizabeth sobbing.

"I'm bringing her to you," Janet told me on the phone. "The fireworks are about to go off, and the traffic is crazy!"

I refused at first, not wanting to put my friend to so much trouble after all she'd already done. But Janet insisted, and I finally relented. "Meet us halfway, then."

An hour and a half later, at a Steak 'n Shake parking lot, my best friend delivered my intoxicated daughter. I didn't know who to hug first! I ordered hamburgers while Will gassed up her car across the street. "I can never thank you enough!" I kept repeating.

Janet drove off. We got home shortly before 3 a.m. I was still wearing my Fourth of July shirt, red with navy blue stars.

The next morning, Will and I prayed, then knocked on the door to Elizabeth's bedroom. I handed her a glass of orange juice, and she sat up in bed. The two of us sat on the wood floor, leaning against her closet doors. He started, "Elizabeth, your mom and I think that—"

> "Because he loves me," says the LORD, "I will rescue him; I will protect him, for he acknowledges my name."
>
> —PSALM 91:14 (NIV)

"I'm not going to rehab!" she interrupted.

We were physically and emotionally exhausted. Still, I sensed a strong divine presence hovering in the room. Peace from above and beyond rested in my weary body. A calm prevailed. We waited.

"I'm not going to rehab! I'm an adult, and you can't make me!" she repeated.

"You're right!" Her dad agreed, then calmly stood up to leave the room. I followed.

"You can call," Elizabeth murmured. I left the room wondering, *What just happened?*

When I called the treatment center, the counselor asked if Elizabeth would be willing to talk, and she agreed. *What changed her mind? More like who! Thank You, God!*

We left for the center after lunch. At 8:30 p.m., two states away, we arrived at the admissions office. Elizabeth barely had more than the clothes on her back. When she opened her purse to get her insurance card, I asked her about the key to her apartment. She looked and looked. It was missing! Yet, she'd had it the night before when she got a Lyft ride. If she'd gotten into her apartment on her own, Janet never would have connected with her. Divine timing!

Today, Elizabeth is sober and lives in an apartment in the same city where she sought treatment. She loves her job and recently went on a mission trip. It's been more than 5 years since God performed that Fourth of July miracle. It wasn't the Easter miracle I'd prayed for, but a grander miracle than I could have imagined. While Elizabeth celebrates milestones on her journey toward freedom from addiction, I celebrate a Holy God who is omnipresent.

A New Definition of Snow Angels

Cynthia A. Lovely

The day started out like any other. I kissed my husband, Dwayne, goodbye on that snowy winter morning as he left for his job at the airport and went about my day.

But while winter storms are common in upstate New York, this one lingered, dumping snow on the streets at such a heavy rate that even the snowplows gave up. I tried not to call Dwayne at work, knowing he was probably busy with his team members in emergency snow ops, trying to keep up with the drifting snow. Eventually he called to let me know his normal shift was turning into a 12-hour shift. His work involved operating heavy-duty snowplow equipment to keep the airport runways clear. To the team's credit, the airport was able to remain open through one of the worst storms in decades. But . . . how was he going to get back home?

At this point, my worrying kicked in. My elderly mother was living with us, and we couldn't afford to lose power and be without heat for any length of time. We did have a generator, but I had no clue how to set it up. My mother and I began to pray in earnest. Finally, my husband finished his shift and started his long trek home through the storm, which had turned into a genuine Northeast blizzard. It was the type of storm where you could barely see the road through the snow, ice and wind—the kind of storm that gave rise to the term "white-out."

Dwayne was driving his 4-wheel drive truck, which was usually dependable in rough weather. However, this storm was beyond what we would normally expect. He kept in touch as much as possible and managed to get to the bottom of the hill that we lived on—5 miles from home—only to hit a snowdrift and get stuck. A local farmer helped him dig out his pickup truck, and he decided to try another route to get home.

He made it as far as the lake at the top of our hill, again only a few miles from home, and then discovered another unplowed road. We kept receiving his updates, and my mother and I continued to pray. He told us he found a few local men who were hanging out in their garage, working on a car. They phoned a friend who had a snowmobile, hoping he would be able to offer help. The man with the snowmobile tried, but he could not get over the huge snowdrifts. Typical of small-town ingenuity, the guys cooked venison hot dogs on a pot-bellied stove while waiting for the plow to come through. I was relieved he had something to eat and a warm place to stay out of the weather. Eventually the plow came by and managed to clear a portion of the road.

His last update described his progress: the five guys piled into a Jeep to attempt the drive down the road to our hill, hoping to get my husband safely back home. They figured if they got stuck, they would have enough manpower to push the Jeep

> The angel of the LORD encamps around those who fear him, and he delivers them.
>
> —PSALM 34:7 (NIV)

free. And they were able to go a couple of miles—until they hit a section where the plow had turned off to a side road. It was back to high snowdrifts blocking the road. At this point my husband made the hard decision to walk the rest of the way. Perhaps not the smartest choice, but he was desperate and worried about us losing power. After his decision, we lost contact with him. What follows is Dwayne's own account of what happened.

When I told the guys who were with me I was going to walk, one of them lent me his hat with earmuffs. I already had on heavy boots and thick gloves. By this time, it was dusk, and the sky was darkening into nightfall. The guys kept the Jeep headlights shining bright on me till I crossed over the next hill out of sight. Suddenly it all went dark. As I lost the light, I realized I was on my own.

In the midst of a blizzard on a lonely country road piled high with snowdrifts, I knew somehow God would see me through. I kept walking, one foot after the other. Some of the drifts were so high I couldn't just walk through them; I had to crawl on my stomach or try to climb over them. I was exhausted from my long shift at work and the tremendous battle to get home through the storm. Was I afraid? Yes! Between my exhaustion and the constant struggle to keep

> **See, I am sending an angel ahead of you to guard you along the way and to bring you to the place I have prepared.**
>
> —EXODUS 23:20 (NIV)

going, I didn't know if I could make it. Yet I knew my wife and mother-in-law were in constant prayer: I added my prayers to theirs with a desperate plea for God's protection.

At one point, when the exhaustion almost got the better of me, I was tempted to give up. All I wanted to do was to sit down in a snowbank and take a rest. But I knew from growing up in the Adirondack area that was a bad idea. You don't quit. You have to keep going. If you stop, you are risking frostbite—or even worse, falling asleep in the snow and not waking up.

That was the point when I started to be truly afraid I'd never make it home. *Lord, I prayed, watch over me. Please help me get back to my family.*

I decided to make a new goal: keep pushing to make it as far as the next house on the road, and hopefully there I could take a break or find temporary shelter.

Just keep walking, I told myself. *One step after another.*

Suddenly, out of nowhere, there was a snowmobile trail in the middle of the road! It gave me hope and the incentive to move forward. Walking on the path made by the snowmobile was much easier, and I knew home was just over the last hill. God was certainly walking with me through this storm. There must have been angels holding me up, because I had no strength left. I think they were New York-trained tough angels with special divine powers!

> **Cast your cares on the Lord and he will sustain you; he will never let the righteous be shaken.**
>
> —PSALM 55:22 (NIV)

I can't even describe how I felt when I finally saw home. All the lights were lit, inside and out, and I knew my family was in there, waiting for me. I pushed my feet to take me that last little bit, and then I was standing on our doorstep. I didn't have to wait long before the door was flung wide open, spilling light into the darkness. The expression on my wife's face was priceless.

I can't even imagine what my face looked like. It was such a relief to see Dwayne finally on our doorstep after all the worrying. And he was a sight—covered with snow, icicles on his hat and hanging from his mustache. It was as if the Abominable Snowman had come in out of the storm.

My mother and I immediately directed him to a shower to defrost. Afterward, we all rejoiced at the blessings we'd received— he had made it home safely, the power never went out, and we were all together. Looking back, we were sure that the Lord had answered our prayers, sending His angels to guide Dwayne home. Truly He is our protection in the worst storms of life!

Mini Miracles on the Cancer Journey

Stephanie A. Wilsey

"It's cancer."

I looked up at my husband. His face reflected the devastation we both felt. While the kids and I were swimming and sunning on this beautiful Georgia beach, he had returned to the hotel. That was when the doctor called with the bad news.

The lump in my 16-year-old daughter's right leg was not supposed to be cancer. Right before leaving for our trip, a specialist at our local children's hospital declared that the baseball-sized lump was very unlikely to be a tumor. It would have to be removed, and he'd biopsy it just in case, but all should be well. Life can change fast, though. Like when you're on a beach with your family and you learn that your daughter has a very rare childhood sarcoma.

Upon hearing her dad's announcement, my daughter, Alexa, looked up at me with her beautiful, big green eyes.

"We're going swimming," I announced.

I don't know how other people react to their child's cancer diagnosis, but I immediately drew my daughter and son into the cool waves. We bobbed up and down as we processed the news while holding hands underneath the water.

When we returned to Pennsylvania, life changed immediately. Alexa started months of radiation treatment, followed by surgical removal of the tumor as well as the entire quadriceps muscle around it. An army of family members took turns taking her on the hour-long daily drive to the hospital. Alexa's Christian school supported her by allowing her to miss two classes for months and also filming them so that she could keep up. Sometimes her classmates added additional humorous videos, and at the end of the year, a teacher and an entire class filmed an entertaining "what you missed" mini-movie that had our family howling in laughter.

After hearing that Alexa's favorite Bible verse was Isaiah 43:2, a kind church friend, who herself understood difficult health diagnoses, printed Alexa's name and Isaiah 43:1–2 on blue wristbands. These wristbands soon made their way throughout the church, Alexa's school, and to numerous friends and family who wore the bands in solidarity with us, acknowledging that God promises to be with us through even the most difficult times. Some said that the bands helped to remind them to pray.

We were so grateful and supported in a time that was so bewildering. How had this happened? Why hadn't this been discovered earlier?

> **But now, this is what the LORD says—he who created you, Jacob, he who formed you, Israel: "Do not fear, for I have redeemed you; I have summoned you by name; you are mine."**
>
> —ISAIAH 43:1 (NIV)

Where are You, God, in all of this? Do You love us?

During this time, well-meaning adults kept telling my daughter that this experience would make her stronger spiritually. This seemed like a lot of extra pressure on her; she not only had to bear with pain and fear but also be a triumphant Christian. While the comments were too ill-timed to be helpful, they did turn out to be true.

> **When you pass through the waters, I will be with you; and when you pass through the rivers, they will not sweep over you. When you walk through the fire, you will not be burned; the flames will not set you ablaze.**
>
> —ISAIAH 43:2 (NIV)

Between the cancer diagnosis and tumor removal, Alexa was cast as Cinderella in her school musical. Neither we nor the musical director knew how long it would take for Alexa to walk, let alone dance, after losing an entire leg muscle. Yet, she would be Cinderella regardless.

Music would prove to be a blessing to Alexa. After she came home from surgery, she went up to her room while I went back downstairs to unpack. Soon, I heard music. Coming back up to investigate, I found her on the floor with her leg carefully stretched in front of her. In her hands was a ukelele, and she was composing a new song—the first of many that she would write over the years. She would later say, "I never felt like writing music until my surgery."

128 | Wrapped *in* His Protection

Within four months of the surgery, she was able to wear her beautiful Cinderella dress, sing, and swirl around in some carefully choreographed movements. Her story was featured in the local newspaper, and she received a special award in a local musical theater competition for an excellent performance through difficult circumstances. She gave a speech giving thanks to God in front of teachers, families, and students. God had indeed worked in her heart and strengthened her.

Before all of this, Alexa was a fairly anxious child, and she was particularly fretful over all things medical. As a toddler, she needed three nurses to hold her down if any needles were present! She later told us that she had always had a great fear of having cancer someday. When your greatest fear comes upon you, you can either give in to that fear or overcome it. Alexa overcame. She endured numerous prods, pokes, needles, treatments, injections, discomforts, and bore it all with a gracious, joy-filled presence. God took away her fear and gave her joy, inexplicable joy.

Many of our friends and family thought that everything would be fine once the tumor was removed. For some people with cancer, this is blessedly true. Yet, cancer is called a "journey" for a reason. For many, cancer looms as a lifelong presence.

We had a sneaking concern that all was not well after the surgery. First, the rareness of this cancer meant that little information was available, and what we did know about this sarcoma was not good. We were in uncharted territory; stages of cancer weren't even assigned for this type. Sure enough, at Alexa's scans in the fall, we learned that the cancer had spread to her lungs, which is typical for patients with her sarcoma. She had nineteen nodules distributed across both lungs.

While the news of a metastatic diagnosis was terrible, God had prepared us during the prior year to rest in Him. We had learned that praying for a miracle does not necessarily translate to God immediately taking away illness. Instead, we saw mini miracles everywhere. We saw miracles in God strengthening Alexa to bear with joy the realization of a lifetime of medical treatment. Other miracles came in God's strengthening of our marriage and His protection of the emotional well-being of our son, who was thriving in middle school. Another involved others realizing that loving us meant keeping us in prayer for many years to come. Our family's approach to the cancer journey was a miracle. From that first impulse to swim and band together, we stayed close during hospital visits, with every visit paired with a nice lunch and, when possible, a library visit for our book-loving daughter. Alexa handled the treatments like a social event—family time in the city with us and socialization hour with her beloved doctors and nursing staff.

God can also work miracles through medical advancements. When Alexa was first diagnosed, no specific treatment was available for her form of cancer. The options were radiation or chemotherapy—both of which had minimal to no effect for this sarcoma—and surgical removal. Even doing a biopsy on the lungs is difficult and painful because it involves deflating the lungs. During my daughter's biopsy, three nodules were removed, but they were the easy ones, located near the edge of her right lung. What would we do with the other sixteen, scattered throughout? Chopping through the lungs each year would not be feasible.

As we pondered the options, our doctor told us, with her face shining, that a new treatment was available. A clinical trial had just wrapped up in the previous month and now a treatment specifically tailored to this sarcoma type was available. My husband and I realized God's grace in the timing. If Alexa's tumor had been diagnosed earlier, she would likely have received painful and unhelpful treatments. Instead, within weeks, a promising new treatment became available—just as she was about to turn 18 and could therefore avoid the difficulties of getting approval for a child to undertake a brand-new medical treatment.

So, while a metastatic cancer diagnosis is one of the worst types of news one can hear, we received it with knowledge of God's grace and blessing. He had provided for her and for us.

As I write this, we are approaching the two-year mark for Alexa's treatment. It hasn't been easy all the way. Right before starting college, she began to experience devastating side effects that harmed her liver, feet, mouth, and stomach. She spent the first two months of college in great pain. She received special accommodations from her school for lateness and absences given that she couldn't walk quickly enough to get to class on time. Every 3 weeks, she'd miss a day of class for treatment. We prayed and felt led to ask the doctors to adjust the treatment to just one immunotherapy medication, rather than two, and her doctors agreed. Since we are in this for the long haul, we are prayerfully pursuing healing, but also life! We want Alexa to have a full life in the present as well as the future.

> [God] comforts us in all our troubles, so that we can comfort those in any trouble with the comfort we ourselves receive from God.
>
> —2 CORINTHIANS 1:4 (NIV)

GOD'S GIFT OF SMELL
— Eryn Lynum —

SOME TREE SPECIES emit certain specific scents when they are under stress. One that we can experience is the Ponderosa pine tree, which smells like vanilla when its bark is scratched, like a scratch-and-sniff sticker. However, many other tree scents are imperceptible to the human nose, yet critical to a forest's health. Some tree species communicate and even warn each other through scent. When a deer nibbles at its branches or an insect infestation arrives, a tree can produce subtle scents to alert other nearby trees, which then produce bitter tannins to ward off predators.

Likewise, God created the community of believers to support and safeguard one another. Spiritual protection is stronger within God's design of faith in fellowship.

God has honored this prayer. Alexa has maintained her treatment regimen and managed to perform in three theater performances and numerous choir concerts. She is currently on tour with a traveling Christian singing group, proclaiming God's word through song and skits. She had her treatment and scans right before the tour and will do it again right after returning.

We may be a family on a cancer journey, but God has granted His grace and sustaining strength through all of it. Our love and joy is palpable, and we are so very thankful. We see His people serving as His hands and feet when they pray for us and support us, and we do the same for others experiencing difficult illnesses.

God's Gracious Gifts
Wendy Lynne Smith

My husband and I were expecting our first boy. After six girls, the imminent arrival of a son truly felt like a miracle. We had already chosen his name: Boaz.

One day, while on a walk with one of my daughters, I asked God for guidance for the time of labor and delivery. I was about 7 months pregnant at the time, and looking forward to the new arrival. *What should I expect this time, Lord?* And like a whisper, the meaning of our son's name raced across my heart: *strong and swift.* I tucked that message deep inside, wondering if the Lord had indeed answered me so quickly and clearly, and how those startling words might prepare me for the time to come. As it happened, my family and I would need a great deal of strength over the coming weeks.

A short time later, I awoke in the dead of night. Had I heard a sound downstairs? I crept out of bed and tiptoed across hardwood floors to the top of the staircase. The lights blazed brightly, illuminating our newly remodeled lower level. As I walked slowly down the stairs, I saw my husband wearing pajama pants and knee-high rubber boots. "What's going on?" I asked. Then I gasped out loud, because as he stepped closer, I could see that our beautiful, expensive carpet was floating as his boots squished into several inches of water with every step. I noticed, for the first time, the sound of a torrential rainfall pouring down outside. But this floor had never flooded that way. Why hadn't the sump pump come on?

I placed my hand protectively on my extended stomach. *Lord, I can't believe this is happening! This baby will be born in a few weeks, and I want our home to be safe when he comes,* I thought. But instead of panic, God's peace wrapped around me. I snapped into action. While my husband carried furniture upstairs, I woke up our teens, who'd been blissfully asleep in their flooding bedroom. We all worked together, and soon, dressers, lamps, books, and toys lined the upstairs hallway, nice and organized. I flapped open a couple of sleeping bags in the upstairs bedrooms, and our teens crawled in. After calling a restoration company, my husband and I headed back to bed for a few more minutes of precious sleep. Morning would come all too quickly.

We spent the next couple weeks working and lining up contractors, as I counted down the days to the baby's birth. We'd lost half of our living space when a twig caused our sump pump to jam. "An act of God," the insurance company concluded. As a result, the damage to our home was not covered by insurance, and we would need to pay for the bulk of the renovation. *Lord, I don't understand, but I know You'll take care of us.* I committed to trusting in my Heavenly Father, who had been my rock and source of comfort throughout my life.

The next day at my prenatal check-up, I told my obstetrician, Dr. Lutz, about our house flood while she measured my stomach and listened to Boaz's heartbeat. I worked part-time as a real estate broker while caring for my growing family. Added to my already busy life and the coming baby, the need for repairs struck me as almost comical. I chuckled wryly.

"Your baby is healthy, and everything looks great. But I'm surprised you can laugh," commented Dr. Lutz.

"It's better to laugh than cry." I was thankful for a loving God who was with me in times of trouble.

After my appointment, I drove straight to the carpet store. In the process of coordinating our home restoration, I had reconnected with one of my friends from high school, whose family owned a wholesale flooring company. As I looked at carpet samples, my phone rang. It was my husband.

"Hi, honey, someone just ran into me. My car's a wreck, but I'm fine."

Losing half our house and a car at the same time? After I ended the call, I said to the company's owner, "My husband just called to tell me not to worry, but that another driver smashed into the side of his car. He's safe, thank God!"

> **"Call to me and I will answer you and tell you great and unsearchable things you do not know."**
>
> —JEREMIAH 33:3 (NIV)

The owner of the flooring company looked at me in surprise, then, without hesitation, prayed boldly for God's provision for every need. He walked me out with encouraging words and the promise that the new carpet would be installed soon.

Please Lord, help us to get the house done before the baby comes, I prayed as I drove home. When I arrived, my husband had already taken his car into the dealership's service center. Because he worked in the automotive industry, he knew that even a car that an insurance company deemed a total loss might still be drivable. Even though the entire side was badly damaged, the door still shut, and the car still ran. The mechanics at the shop confirmed that the car was still mechanically sound and safe to drive. What a blessing! We couldn't have afforded to replace the car just then. A warm feeling enveloped me as I praised God for His gracious gifts. His peace and provision were evident as we faced each challenge.

The next week, my mom and I took one of my daughters to high tea for her fourteenth birthday. I told my mom about the stomach flu that had been going around our family. "We've been healthy for a week, so I think it might finally be over."

My mom looked at me with concern. "Have you gotten it yet?"

"Well, this flu could prompt early labor, and we've already been through so much," I replied. "I have to keep trusting God to take care of my baby and me."

"True," my mom agreed. "Don't worry. I believe everything will be fine."

But the next day, my husband became ill. He'd been the strong one, taking care of each child in turn, while I had tried to isolate to protect our unborn little one. I hoped the isolation would keep us healthy, but the next week, the flu finally came for me.

My husband found Dr. Lutz's phone number and contacted her to let her know what had happened. She prescribed a safe anti-nausea medicine, and I took some and went to bed. But then contractions began, maybe one or two per hour. My husband took care of me throughout the early morning hours. When his alarm went off, I encouraged him to go to work.

"Are you sure?" he asked, troubled, tucking the quilt around me gently.

"Yes, I'm sure. It's too early for the baby to come. Besides, our house isn't finished yet." My eyes closed automatically, and I drifted off to sleep once more.

But after a few hours, I was awakened by strong contractions, which were now happening about every twenty minutes.

I called Dr. Lutz again, and she said I might have become dehydrated from the flu. "You could try drinking more fluids, or you can go to the hospital, and they can give you fluids through an IV," she said.

Unsure what to do, I called my friend Melissa. After I explained the situation, she asked, "Do you want me to pick you up and drive you to the hospital?"

"No," I answered. "My doctor told me to go in if needed, but I don't think it's needed."

Silence.

Then, with concern, she said, "I think you should go. Now!"

"Oh," I replied, nonplussed. "Well, I can call my husband to come home from work. He's closer than you are, and then we'll go to the hospital."

> God is our refuge and strength, an ever-present help in trouble.
>
> —PSALM 46:1 (NIV)

My friend's wise advice turned out to be yet another proof of God's constant provision. As I forced myself to get out of bed, my water broke. This baby was coming, whether I was ready or not! I called out instructions to my teenage daughters, and they raced to my aid, gathering things for the baby and me into an overnight bag.

By the time my husband got home, I was ready to go. I carefully laid down in the back seat, and he wildly raced across town to the hospital. Unbeknownst to me, my husband had again reached out to let my doctor know that my water had broken. Enjoying a morning walk, Dr. Lutz then began sprinting home. She jumped into her vehicle and headed to the hospital, hoping to get there in time.

What followed was straight out of a TV drama. Upon arriving at the birth center, I laid my head on the counter. "I don't think I can do this anymore," I said. "I need my epidural."

The nurses looked at each other dubiously, and I heard one murmur, "Her doctor called ahead. But she's a month early. We'll probably have to send her home."

A nurse gently guided me to a bed in the evaluation room, and I heard the words, "Ten plus, the head is coming!"

Tears filled my eyes. I was about to meet my baby boy! God's whispered answer to my prayer came to mind. *Strong and swift*. Peace filled my heart. In tandem, nurses pushed my hospital bed while sprinting down zigzagging hallways. Within minutes, a healthy baby boy was born.

Just after his birth, my doctor entered the room. "You came!" I exclaimed.

> Consider it pure joy, my brothers and sisters, whenever you face trials of many kinds, because you know that the testing of your faith produces perseverance.
>
> —JAMES 1:2–3 (NIV)

Dr. Lutz smiled and said, "I was afraid I would be too late!"

"You're just in time to take care of me," I said gratefully as a few more tears slipped down my cheeks. "Thank you so much for coming."

Though a month early, our son was in perfect health. While I was recovering in the hospital, the new carpet was installed, and my thoughtful teenagers moved all the furniture back and set up their bedrooms. I cried tears of happiness when I arrived home with our new son to a finished house. In the next month, two real estate deals closed, giving us the exact amount of money needed to pay for the reconstruction. God's gracious gifts of a divine word, kind friend, and dedicated doctor whispered of God's constant presence in our lives.

Walking in Faith and Prayer

Stacy Leicht

As our car reached the outer limits of the neighborhood after a two-week family vacation, I was itching to go swimming in the neighborhood pool and to see my best friend, who I was sure would be there on a hot summer day. My mom reminded me to be patient; we needed to unpack the car. But I was 7 years old, so of course I continued to pester her.

"Can I please go swimming?" I begged.

"Give me a few minutes to finish unpacking, then we can go," Mom said.

Shortly after unpacking the trunk, Mom told me to put on my bathing suit. We headed toward the pool. Running ahead, I found my best friend waiting for me. We hugged and began walking toward the pool.

Moments later, I heard loud screams. It took a few seconds to realize it was me. My feet were sinking into freshly poured hot tar. I'd been so excited about going to the pool that I hadn't even noticed the hot patch in front of me, and there were no warning signs—no tape marking off the area, no workers nearby to warn people off. There was nothing to stop me from putting my feet into the burning tar until it was too late. The pain was excruciating, and I could smell my flesh burning.

A lady began running toward me. I learned later she was a nurse. She gently lifted me from the tar and ran toward the pool. "I've got you; I've got you," she repeated frantically as she ran toward the water. The fiery liquid sizzled on my feet as the tar continued to burn. My screams were loud enough to get the attention of all of the guests at the pool.

"Hold on!" she told me. When she dunked my feet over the edge of the pool, steam began rising from the water. Even as I continued to yell, I noticed the fear in the eyes of the people around me.

The clock was ticking; I would need to go to the hospital to have the tar removed, because the hot, sticky substance would keep burning my skin as long as it was touching me.

> "Don't be afraid. I will provide for you and your children." And he reassured them and spoke kindly to them.
>
> —GENESIS 50:21 (NIV)

My mom returned quickly with our car and a few people loaded me into the front seat so I could hold my feet up by the air conditioner vents. The pain was so intense my stomach felt sick. I could smell the horrible stench of burning flesh.

"You'll be OK," Mom said over and over. Was she talking to herself or me? Her voice quavered as she spoke. Even as I screamed I looked to her for reassurance that I would indeed be fine. She kept her eyes on the road, focused on getting me to the emergency room as soon as possible.

As soon as we arrived at the hospital, nurses and doctors hustled to take care of me. A group of doctors looked at my feet. The one who seemed to be in charge spoke to the people around us, looked at me at length, then turned to the nurse and whispered something. Then he turned and smiled back at me, saying with a wink, "We'll take good care of you."

The nurse inserted an IV quickly into my arm, then pushed medicine into the IV. The medicine took effect quickly, and I closed my eyes.

The next few hours at the hospital were critical. I woke up in a burn unit after the doctors had performed a procedure to remove the tar from my feet. I had suffered third-degree burns on the bottoms and parts of the tops of my feet. I had a great deal of healing to do.

> He will cover you with his feathers, and under his wings you will find refuge; his faithfulness will be your shield and rampart.
>
> —PSALM 91:4 (NIV)

I had expected to spend my summer swimming and biking with friends, but instead I had to lie in a hospital bed with my feet covered in salve and wrapped in thick bandages. Pain and fear blanketed my thoughts. I had so many questions. How long would I have to stay here? Would I be able to walk again? The doctors said it would take time, but how much time?

Unable to even get out of bed by myself, I was totally dependent on my parents' care. Weeks became months, and frustration became the norm. I tired of lying in bed day after day. I didn't have a TV in my bedroom like most people do now. I had books, stuffed animals, coloring books, and some activities a few neighbor families dropped off for me. Although I appreciated their kindness, the days were long, and the pain was hard to bear. I could hear my friends' voices outside as they rode bikes down the street, jumped rope, and played tag, and I longed to be outside playing with them.

As time passed, fear began to take hold. I wondered if I would be able to walk, run, and play with my friends in the same ways I had before. I was missing swim, ballet, and tap-dance lessons, and school was about to begin again. It would be 7 long months before my recovery began. There was very little skin left on the bottoms of my feet, and it had to regrow before I could get up and walk. It was even longer before I could run or dance or play. My Christian parents spoke of God's love and protection for me. Every evening before bed, my parents would pray over me.

> Rejoice always, pray continually, give thanks in all circumstances; for this is God's will for you in Christ Jesus.
>
> —1 THESSALONIANS 5:16–18 (NIV)

I heard their prayers and wondered if God would heal my feet. My parents had certainty in their voices when they prayed to God. Their belief that my feet would heal did not waver. There was something about hearing their prayers that gave me peace, and I felt a deep sense of love as I listened to the words they spoke each night. They prayed for healing and gave thanks that the burns were not worse. They expressed gratitude to God for the doctors and nurses who performed amazing medical procedures and for their quick thinking and actions. I prayed too, not because my relationship with God was strong, but because my parents modeled how to pray.

In the middle of the night, if I awoke in pain, I would pray. Many times, I would feel relief as I said the words. As the months wore on, I came to genuinely believe that God would heal me, and, after months of prayer, He did.

The smell of freshly poured tar is still a trigger for me. Passing construction sites or road work is difficult. I have learned to pray before long trips, and to ask God to be by my side if I encounter my biggest fear. Not only has God helped me during my car rides, but His constant presence keeps me from getting physically sick.

To this day, my feet are always in shoes because my feet are very tender. Walking on tough or hard surfaces can be very uncomfortable. But I can walk, and God's love for me is evident with every step I take. I am grateful for the gift of parents who taught me to pray at an early age and the care and protection of the One who healed me.

God Is Always on Call
Elizabeth Erlandson

Tap, tap, tap. The rhythmic sound of Doug's cane kept pace with my steps as we walked across the mall parking lot. We had just enjoyed a rare outing—lunch at Applebee's to celebrate our forty-second wedding anniversary—and were returning to our car. Focused on getting to the car and opening the door for Doug, I didn't notice when the tapping stopped.

And then I heard my husband cry out, "Help me, Elizabeth!"

My husband suffers from PDA (peripheral artery disease), which has resulted in two life-threatening ruptures, several surgeries, months of rehabilitation, balance issues, and memory loss. You might think a person would become used to dealing with medical emergencies, but each one brings a new round of panic, fear, and worry.

Doug's cane had caught in a rut and he lay sprawled on the blacktop. No way would I be able to lift him by myself! What if something were broken? Or maybe he was bleeding—a major worry, since Doug is on blood thinners.

I scanned the parking lot searching for help, but no one was in sight. Panicked, I breathed a quick prayer. "Lord, help us."

Better call 911, I thought. I fished my cell phone out of my purse but before I could punch in the numbers, help arrived. Three EMTs on their way to lunch had spotted Doug on the ground and me hovering over him.

Two men carried him back to our car while the other technician retrieved his medical bag from the ambulance. He took Doug's blood pressure, listened to his heart, cleaned and bandaged his scraped knees, and assured us that nothing was broken. "Ice your knees when you get home and rest," he advised.

The EMT waved off my offer to pay for his services and assured me that he was just doing his job. But I knew it was no coincidence they had been there at just the right time—it was God's provision.

This wasn't the first time help had arrived just when it was needed. Time and again, I have witnessed God's provision at critical moments—like last October, when four neighbors just happened to be leaving for work when Doug fell on our driveway. They carried him into our house and made sure he was OK. One of our neighbors gave me his phone number in case I needed additional help.

Another time when Doug was ready to be released from a rehab facility, I needed a few strong men to rearrange our furniture to accommodate his walker. I fretted, wondering how we would manage. Then, without my asking, one of the elders in our church stopped by to visit Doug and offered to help in whatever way he could. He arranged to have the extra furniture removed and donated to a local charity.

One crisis, however, stands out above the others. Even though it happened 19 years ago, I still recall every detail with clarity. Doug and I had switched from using a landline to cell service, but we kept our old phones plugged in. We had a working number because the phone service came "bundled" with our cable TV and internet access. By keeping the landline, we paid less.

The phone in our bedroom was a clunky, cream-colored desk model that we shoved under the bed. It rang at inopportune times, and the calls were always from a solicitor or a wrong number. We talked about ditching it, but it still sat on the floor, a technological dinosaur.

A few days after our most recent conversation about the phone, I attended my first Pilates class. Doug and I usually eat dinner together, but that night, I prepared his meal and left it on the counter. When I arrived home an hour and a half later, the food was still on the counter. I called his name, but he didn't answer.

Doug is conscientious. I knew he wouldn't have left the house without writing me a note. Hesitantly, I walked into the living room.

> **He sent out his word and healed them; he rescued them from the grave.**
>
> —PSALM 107:20 (NIV)

Bits of paper were scattered on the carpet and there was a hole in the wall near the front door. *Someone broke into our house!*

Dread gripped me. I wanted to run, to do something, but I was trapped by the worry running through my mind. What had they done to Doug? What if they were still in the house, hiding and waiting for me?

My hands shook as I called my best friend, Ardith, and told her what I had encountered. "Contact the police now," she said. "I'll be right over."

While we were on the phone, the landline rang. It was the hospital. Doug had suffered a ruptured aneurysm in his left iliac artery and was bleeding internally. Even though it was already evening, a vascular surgeon had just completed a scheduled operation when Doug was wheeled into the ER. By the time I arrived at the hospital, my husband was in surgery. It took 6 hours to repair the rupture, but Doug survived and healed more quickly than expected.

> **Before they call I will answer; while they are still speaking I will hear.**
>
> —ISAIAH 65:24 (NIV)

I later learned that he had gone into the master bathroom to wash up for dinner when he felt excruciating pain in his left leg, right below the hip. He crawled out of the bathroom and lay on the bed, hoping the pain would subside, but it worsened. Thinking that a hard surface would be better than a soft mattress, he slid to the floor, but the pain increased and he lost feeling in both legs and one arm.

Doug hates to make phone calls, and he rarely asks for help, but he had no alternative. Now on the floor, he could see the old phone, still plugged in. He called me and got voicemail. Next, he called Ardith, but she was with me. Finally, desperate for help, he dialed 911.

Our front door was locked, so the EMTs forced it open, which created the hole in the wall. The pieces of paper were wrapping from tubes and syringes. Despite his pain, Doug remained alert throughout the entire ordeal, including the ambulance ride to the hospital. He recalls having the CT scan and how, after reviewing the results, the emergency room staff shifted into high gear. He even remembers the doctor telling him he would die if they didn't fix him and his replying, "Then fix me."

Thankfully, they did fix him. Since then, he has experienced many health-related emergencies, like the recent fall in the parking lot, but in every situation, help arrived precisely when we needed it.

God knew that Doug would need that old phone. Thanks to our procrastination and heavenly providence, that cream-colored landline became a precious lifeline and a reminder that whenever I need help, all I have to do is call. The Lord always answers.

When I stand before thee
at the day's end, thou shalt
see my scars and know
that I had my wounds
and also my healing.

—Rabindranath Tagore

CHAPTER 4

Sustained and Healed

God's Promise and Sarah's Laughter 152
    Kelsey Green

The Solid Rock 158
    Rebecca D. Bruner

The Baby Is Stronger than Anyone Knows 166
    Cecil Taylor

God Is Forming You 171
    Heidi Chiavaroli

God Sees in the Dark 177
    Jeanne Takenaka

A Miracle Worth Remembering 183
    Lori Tanabe

Grace for the Long Haul 189
    Carolyn Waverly

Hope for the Future 195
    Mindy Baker

Reassurance During a Time of Silence 199
    Barbara Latta

God's Promise and Sarah's Laughter

Kelsey Green

As I made the long drive to work from yet another doctor's appointment, I felt broken and desperate. My husband and I were 3 years into a season of infertility. During that time, we had suffered multiple miscarriages and depleted our savings account. I had learned how to give myself injectable medications and how to reroute a conversation when asked, "So, do you want children?" We had completed the expensive and complicated IVF process after nothing else had worked, but I was quickly running out of faith that any of these efforts would result in a baby.

I had become pregnant with one of our precious embryos just a few months before this time, and it had resulted in another miscarriage. The first few appointments for that baby had gone well, and I felt hopeful that we were finally on our way to growing our family. That hope was lost during the last scheduled appointment at the fertility clinic. I didn't realize how deep emotional pain could go until I heard the doctor somberly say, "I'm sorry, we can't find a heartbeat." I became sad and numb in a way that I had never experienced before. Grief invaded my heart and followed me around like a black storm cloud. I didn't know how to relate to our friends or family anymore, and I had trouble finding joy in anything at all. Everything felt so wrong.

God felt the most wrong of all. I grew up knowing that God had good plans for my life and that He loved and cared for me. I had always accepted these claims, but this long trial of suffering, tears, prayers, and silence from God had me doubting my beliefs. On that day, as I drove to work, I could feel myself running out of hope and turning away from trusting in my Creator.

I turned on a Christian radio station and began to sing and pray the worship songs over myself. I wasn't sure when I had started this practice, but it had become my ritual driving to and from the fertility clinic appointments. I was less than 5 minutes away from my office and could feel despair taking over my spirit. I was about to start another day of a life that I didn't care about, with a God that I thought no longer cared about me. As I resigned myself to the resentment, I heard the radio DJ announce the verse of the day, Isaiah 43:19: "For I am about to do something new. See, I have already begun! Do you not see it? I will make a pathway through the wilderness. I will create rivers in the dry wasteland" (NLT).

> Consider it pure joy, my brothers and sisters, whenever you face trials of many kinds, because you know that the testing of your faith produces perseverance.
>
> —JAMES 1:2–3 (NIV)

The world seemed to stop. *What did I just hear?* The words shot through me, straight to my heart, and I knew in my soul that they came directly from God. Was He talking to me out loud? Did I make those words up? Why did this moment feel so different from every other one that morning? I didn't understand what had happened: I had never experienced something like this before.

A few moments later, when I pulled into my office parking lot, I looked up the verse on my phone. Sure enough, it was in fact a very real part of Scripture. Isaiah had prophesied it over 2,000 years earlier, and here I was receiving that very same word from God.

I read that scripture, that promise, many times that day. I could not believe how my heart had jolted hearing His words that morning. Why would He give this gift of assurance to me, and what did it even mean? Was I going to finally have a pregnancy that resulted in a baby? Were my husband and I going to adopt? Was I going to have joy again even if my life didn't include a child? I didn't know the answers, but I felt that promise from God sink into my soul and soften my desperate and hopeless heart.

A month later, we completed another single embryo transfer. An at-home test confirmed that I was pregnant again, but I couldn't allow myself to get excited. My heart was too guarded to be optimistic. I knew the overwhelming pain of disappointment and had learned to expect it.

A few days after that positive pregnancy test, I started to feel sick. I developed a fever and became very dehydrated. My husband was adamant about taking me to a local outpatient clinic. I was visibly pale and weak, and I shared that I was also newly pregnant. The provider recommended that I go to the emergency room to receive fluids for dehydration, just as an extra precaution because of the pregnancy. I insisted that my husband stay home. I saw no reason for both of us to spend our afternoon bored at the hospital.

As I sat in the emergency room, I thought sarcastically to myself, *What a great start for this baby!* I was tired, grumpy, and felt certain that this illness had already compromised the pregnancy. After a few hours, the emergency room physician ordered an ultrasound; she wanted to confirm that I was still pregnant. My heart sank immediately, and everything felt heavy. I had been here before. The anxiety started and I began to emotionally ready myself for a new round of grief.

I was sent into a dark and uninviting imaging room with the technician. We both looked as if we didn't want to be there. We engaged in some small talk as she prepared me for the scan. I remember wondering if this pregnancy—and my half-hearted hope—was about to end. The procedure began, and I could feel the dread creep through my body.

Then she asked, cautiously, "Are you sure you didn't transfer two embryos?"

Once again, the world seemed to stop. *What did I just hear?* My mind felt out of focus, and an unfamiliar warmth spread through my chest. I sat up, uttering a shaky and incredulous "No." Even though my brain was already starting to make sense of what it had heard, I needed her to say the words. "Why did you ask me that?"

> **For I am about to do something new. See, I have already begun! Do you not see it? I will make a pathway through the wilderness. I will create rivers in the dry wasteland.**
>
> —ISAIAH 43:19 (NLT)

She turned the screen to face me. "Because I see two babies here."

I stared at the imaging screen. My eyes were seeing two, tiny, barely visible embryos. I could not make sense of the situation. How should I reconcile the pain of the last few years with the emotions of this moment? It felt complicated and confusing. Why was I pregnant with these miracle babies? And could I survive the grief if this pregnancy ended like all the others had?

> Then the LORD said to Abraham, "Why did Sarah laugh and say, 'Will I really have a child, now that I am old?' Is anything too hard for the LORD? I will return to you at the appointed time next year, and Sarah will have a son."
>
> —GENESIS 18:13–14 (NIV)

I finished up in the emergency room and tried to mentally prepare myself to share this news with my husband. He had called twice as I was being discharged, but I hadn't answered. How could I tell him over the phone what had just happened?

I slid into my car, still overwhelmed, and started to drive home. I decided to pull over at a gas station to try to process the last hour of my life.

The technician's question was still ringing in my ears: "Are you sure you didn't transfer two embryos?" Yes, I was sure it had been only one embryo. And yet somehow one had turned into two. I had been praying and hoping for one single baby for years, and now I was pregnant with two of them. I was in such disbelief and joy that I laughed out loud at the situation and at God.

In that instant, I pictured Sarah from the Old Testament. Sarah had been 90 years old when the Lord told her husband, Abraham, that she would have a baby. When Sarah heard this promise, she found it so unbelievable that she laughed out loud. That story of a faithful God doing impossible things had now come to life for me. I sat in my car with uncertainty, humility, and gratitude toward my God.

I managed to get home that afternoon and share the news with my husband. To say we were both in disbelief would be an understatement.

We later found out that our single embryo had split soon after the transfer, resulting in a pregnancy with identical twins. I wish I could say from that point on that I confidently and willingly trusted in God and His plans, but that wouldn't be the truth. I still struggled with worry and fear that something was going to go wrong. But as my pregnant body began to transform, I could feel God slowly repairing my broken and desperate heart. He had changed something in me. I could feel and trust in His sovereignty over my family. I was convinced and secure in knowing that these two babies were a blessing from Him and for Him. His promise and provision over their lives was made clear to me from those very first moments in that emergency room when I learned that one embryo had become two.

I write this as a mom of 4-year-old twin boys with copper-red hair and a passion for dinosaurs. Emmett Asher and Miles David are constant reminders of the happiness and love that God poured out onto us through their births. They are lovable, loud, joyful and without a doubt a blessing from God. Second only to Jesus, they are the greatest gift that God has ever given me.

The Solid Rock
Rebecca D. Bruner

The X-ray tech came out to find me in the hallway. "Where was your melanoma?" she asked.

"On my right thigh," I responded. "Then I had a recurrence in my groin lymph nodes about 4 years ago."

"There was nothing in your lungs?" she asked.

Puzzled, I shook my head. "No."

In the years that I had been coming in for routine cancer screenings, no tech had ever asked me such a question. Generally, they ran tests and left it to the doctors to interpret the results. The fact that she had spoken with me about my medical history felt like a bad sign.

I tried to put it out of my mind. I was a busy mom with two young children, a seven-year-old girl and four-year-old boy. The original melanoma had been surgically removed from my thigh in a wide-area excision when my daughter was one year old. During my pregnancy with my son, I had discovered a lump on that same upper thigh, so 20 weeks into my second pregnancy, I had another cancer surgery. The surgeon removed all ten lymph nodes from my right groin area, but only one was cancerous. By God's grace, the cancer in the affected node had swelled to a palpable lump without spreading to any of the other lymph nodes in the region.

After giving birth to my son, I went through a year of interferon therapy. It was a hard treatment. Interferon is the product of the body's own immune system that causes flu-like symptoms, and interferon therapy was like living with the flu for a year. I had mega-dose infusions in the oncologist's office 5 days a week for the first 4 weeks. After that, I had to give myself interferon injections three nights a week. If I didn't premedicate with Tylenol and Benadryl, I'd wind up with 102-degree fevers, along with chills so bad my body shook. Since the end of that treatment, there had been no further sign of any cancer.

"Based on the original location of your melanoma," my oncologist, Dr. Chassen, had explained, "the major organs we will need to watch for signs of metastasis are your lungs and your liver."

So every 6 months I went in for chest X-rays and bloodwork. Once a year, I would get a CT scan. At my follow-up appointments, the doctor would palpate my liver, feel the lymph nodes in my neck and armpits, listen to my lungs, and give me the results of all my tests.

This time, he walked into the exam room carrying my chart. "Your blood work looks fine, but your chest X-ray was abnormal. You've got a spot on your left lung."

> I waited patiently for the LORD; he turned to me and heard my cry. He lifted me out of the slimy pit, out of the mud and mire; he set my feet on a rock and gave me a firm place to stand.
>
> —PSALM 40:1–2 (NIV)

I swallowed hard.

"This is typically the kind of thing we would just watch," he explained, "but considering your history I'm recommending an open biopsy."

"What does that mean?"

"It means you need to have surgery. Instead of just trying to extract some cells with a needle, the surgeon will cut your lung open and remove the lesion. It will be sent to pathology while you are still on the operating table. If it's malignant, the surgeon will remove more lung tissue to ensure that the borders are clean."

I nodded. In the back of my mind, I reviewed what I already knew. When I had the wide-area excision of the original melanoma from my thigh, it had been deep. The cancer had penetrated through all the superficial skin layers down to the dermis. The oncologist had called that stage two. When it had come back in the groin lymph nodes adjacent to the original site, that had been stage three. If the spot on my lung turned out to be cancer, I knew it would be stage four—distant metastasis to a vital organ. The final stage.

The doctor told me he wanted to run some additional tests. In a daze, I returned to the lobby and waited for the phlebotomist to call me in. Desperate to reach my husband, I attempted to call him at work.

His phone rang. Once, twice, three times. "You have reached the office of Stewart Bruner . . ." the recorded message droned.

I hung up without leaving a message. A lump formed in my throat. I blinked back tears. I was only 32 years old. Wasn't cancer an old person's disease? Young mothers weren't supposed to die of cancer.

This treacherous new curve on the road of my cancer journey unnerved me, yet my fear had very little to do with the prospect of my own death. If I were to die, I was confident that I would go to heaven to be with Jesus. But the thought of leaving behind my two sweet babies and my beloved husband struck terror in my heart. How would they manage?

My fear was magnified by the fact that my grandmother had lost her own mother when she was very young. I had grown up hearing the sad tales of how Grandma's life had never been the same after her mother died. Grandma had been a girl of nine. Her mother had been 33, scarcely older than I was.

By the time Grandma reached her teens, she was already caring single-handedly for her younger siblings. Miserable, she decided to run away from home, assume a new identity, and seek a job as a nanny. Her plan might have succeeded if her younger sister hadn't tattled on her.

> "For how can I bear to see disaster fall on my people? How can I bear to see the destruction of my family?"
>
> —ESTHER 8:6 (NIV)

Knowing her story, I wondered, *how could children who've lost their mother ever flourish or find joy?* Such thoughts filled my heart with despair for my little ones.

Days passed, and one by one, every possibility other than cancer was eliminated. The likelihood that the spot on my lung was malignant loomed larger.

I had been reading the Bible's account of Esther during all this. On this reading I was struck by how Esther's entire story pivots on the 3-day fast that precedes her bold appearance before the king. Esther tells her cousin Mordecai to have all the

Jews in the city of Susa fast for her, neither eating nor drinking. She and her maidens fast in the same way.

I knew fasting was something you were supposed to do when you desperately needed God's favor in a perilous situation, like the one Esther had faced. The threat of stage-four cancer and the prospect of dying and leaving behind two young children certainly felt perilous. I began a fast of my own.

For the three days and nights leading up to my CT scan, I ate nothing. I drank only water. During the fast, I cried out to God. "Please don't take my life," I pleaded. "Let me live to raise my children, to see them grow up."

I felt weak, anxious, and exhausted. I had very little energy and no sense of assurance that my requests were really getting through to God.

Finally, the morning of the CT scan dawned. I broke my fast. I will never forget how good the oat bran muffins tasted that morning. Then, I took a shower.

Warm water poured over me. God's voice was clear as he spoke to my very soul. *Will you trust Me to work all things together for good, not just in your life, but in your children's lives?*

Yes, Lord.

What if that means losing you to cancer? Can you trust that I will work even that together for good?

Yes, Lord.

No matter what I allow in their lives, I will work it together for their ultimate good. I won't take you from them unless and until that is the VERY BEST thing.

Throughout my fast, I had been desperate for assurance that I would not die of cancer. What God showed me instead was that He was infinitely good and infinitely trustworthy.

From the moment I'd learned about the spot on my lung, I'd lost my footing. I'd felt my heart slipping, sinking down into the muck. Now, I realized my heart had reached the bedrock of God's goodness. I stood secure upon the solid rock.

With this profound, supernatural sense of assurance and peace, I went in for the CT scan.

Several weeks later, on the morning of my surgery, my husband and I made our way to the hospital pre-op area. I changed out of my clothes and into a gown made of dark blue crepe paper. It came complete with a funny, plastic strip to tie around my waist. I plaited my hair into one long braid, not wanting to risk throwing up on my hair while coming out of anesthesia.

> "Go, gather together all the Jews who are in Susa, and fast for me. Do not eat or drink for three days, night or day. I and my attendants will fast as you do. When this is done, I will go to the king, even though it is against the law."
>
> —ESTHER 4:16 (NIV)

Nurses came and checked my vitals, then started an IV. While we were waiting for the anesthesiologist and lung surgeon to arrive, the assistant pastor and the lead pastor of my church showed up. God had laid it on both their hearts to come and pray with us prior to my surgery.

We spent time praying and praising God for His goodness. We expressed our trust in His ability to heal, but also in His wisdom. I knew I could trust Him completely, regardless. Even

GOD'S GIFT OF TOUCH
— Linda L. Kruschke —

QUEEN ESTHER FOUND herself in an impossible situation. Her people, the Israelites, were sentenced to die by royal edict. She had to speak to the king, but by approaching him she risked her own life if he was displeased. "When he saw Queen Esther standing in the court, he was pleased with her and held out to her the gold scepter that was in his hand. So Esther approached and touched the tip of the scepter" (Esther 5:2, NIV). Christians don't need to fear for their lives if they approach God's throne. They can reach out and touch Him in their time of need.

---

if I had stage-four cancer, I knew He would not leave me or forsake me, and that He would work out every detail for the good of my husband and children, as well as myself.

Eventually, the wait was over. They wheeled my bed into the surgical suite and administered the anesthesia.

I remember waking in the recovery room. As I fought to regain consciousness, everything around me looked blurry. Groggy as I was, my surgeon was bursting to tell me the outcome of the biopsy. "The spot on your lung was a granuloma. It wasn't cancer. It was nothing but scar tissue."

I'm sure no woman has ever been happier to have had unnecessary surgery than I was that day!

Yet, from a spiritual perspective, this ordeal had been very necessary. Through it, God had taught me to trust Him more unconditionally than I ever had before. I'd learned from the experience that I could rely on His goodness and unfailing love. God's good heart for me is the solid rock on which I am firmly planted, when all life's circumstances are sinking sand.

The Baby Is Stronger Than Anyone Knows
Cecil Taylor

The baby is stronger than anyone knows.
    That voice. I had heard it in my head a few times before, and I believed it to be the voice of the Holy Spirit. Each of these spirit messages had been followed by something amazing. And I needed something amazing in this moment, because although I didn't know it at the time, the lives of my wife and my soon-to-be-born baby were in jeopardy.
    The evening before, I had rushed my pregnant, diabetic wife, Sara, to the emergency room. This was many years ago, and at that time any diabetic pregnancy was considered high-risk. Sudden swings in blood sugar put a heavy strain not only on the mother but also on the developing baby, potentially leading to organ failure or even failure of multiple systems in the body. Throughout her pregnancy, Sara had been experiencing nausea, aches, and sleeping issues; now in her eighth month, she was near total exhaustion, constantly scratching an insatiable itch that prevented her from sleeping. She kept repeating, "This baby is killing me!" I thought, but didn't say aloud, that I had never seen someone experiencing a living hell like this.
    The night before, her speech had started to slur, and when I took her to the emergency room, the staff member admitting

us asked, "Did you know that you're yellow?" The change had been so gradual that neither of us had noticed: Sara had jaundice. They admitted her immediately and began running tests. I returned home to care for our 2-year-old son, bracing for what might come next.

We trusted the man governing her care, Dr. T, the best high-risk obstetrician in the area. Dr. T had delivered only the most endangered babies for 15 years—including our firstborn—and never lost one. Dr. T had seen his own share of trouble; his father was also a physician, serving government officials in Iran. When the ruling regime fell in 1979, his family fled to the United States as Ayatollah Khomeini returned from exile to take power. Yes, Dr. T had been tested by tough scrapes, so we were confident in him.

> **Let the wise listen and add to their learning, and let the discerning get guidance.**
>
> —PROVERBS 1:5 (NIV)

The next morning, I called Sara's hospital room. No answer. Worried, I kept myself distracted by cleaning the kitchen while I waited. I called her room again. No answer. I continued to pray as I started folding laundry.

It was while I was folding laundry that the voice spoke: *The baby is stronger than anyone knows.*

At first I wasn't sure what to make of the message. Then it came again, leaving me confused but oddly steadied. The voice repeated the same words periodically until my phone rang about 30 minutes later, and then things began to blur.

Sara answered, her voice rushed and quivering. Her liver was failing, but her deepest concern was for the baby, because the test results indicated the baby was about to die. Dr. T said mother and baby must be separated. With Sara's second cesarean section beginning soon, it was time to leap in the car and drive 25 minutes to the hospital.

On this clear day, I needed wipers for my eyes as I drove. The voice accompanied me, reiterating, *The baby is stronger than anyone knows.* I clung to those words like a drowning swimmer clutching a life preserver, hanging on to the only hope I had, trusting the Spirit knew what was going to happen.

> **And he took the children in his arms, placed his hands on them and blessed them.**
>
> —MARK 10:16 (NIV)

I said the phrase aloud a few times, my words echoing the Spirit's mantra as I tried to reassure myself.

I reached the hospital just in time. I scrubbed, dressed in an attendant's gown, and joined the crew preparing Sara in the delivery room.

The anesthesiologist had inserted an epidural drip into Sara's back to prevent pain. A few moments remained before the doctors would begin the C-section. Dr. T took the opportunity to revisit our mutual decision to tie Sara's tubes to prevent future pregnancies. "I don't think I should tie the tubes," he told us. "I think you ought to wait on that procedure."

"Why?" I asked.

Then his ominous words: "Because I don't think I can save this baby."

Startled, we agreed. Dr. T walked away, leaving us shattered in his wake. Our hearts sank to our stomachs, and we sobbed aloud as we held hands. The obstetrician who had flawlessly handled the most dire delivery situations for 15 years was telling us that our baby was likely to die. We trusted him. Now what hope was there?

Then I remembered. There indeed was hope.

Leaning over Sara lying on the delivery table, I told her, "It's going to be OK. God told me earlier that the baby is stronger than anyone knows. God assured me it will turn out all right." Remembering my prior encounters with the Holy Spirit, Sara believed. We began to experience a peace that calmed us in the midst of fear.

It wasn't long before the baby's head poked out. Because the baby's lungs were filled with meconium, Dr. T extracted fluid from the mouth and nose. Then with a "1, 2, 3," Dr. T and his assisting physician pulled the baby out into the world.

> **You will be secure, because there is hope; you will look about you and take your rest in safety.**
>
> —JOB 11:18 (NIV)

The baby was a boy. If nothing else, our baby now had a name: Austin.

A whirlwind of activity commenced, the doctors whisking Austin to a side table, Austin crying faintly but persistently—then more drama unfolding on our side of the room with Sara struggling to breathe, feeling a crushing weight in her chest and pain in her right arm.

Later she would describe to me how, with everyone paying attention to Austin and without the breath to speak, she thought, *I'm going to die on this delivery table, and no one will notice!* Then the anesthesiologist noticed Sara's EKG readings and called for her transfer to the cardiac emergency unit. The medical team allowed Sara and me a quick glance at our precious boy before Austin was rushed to the neonatal intensive care unit (NICU), Sara was wheeled to cardiac care at the other end of the hospital, and I was left between them, calling my church to request a minister to sit in vigil with me.

After some time, the cardiologist reported that Sara had not experienced a heart attack, and she was returned to the maternity recovery ward. Meanwhile, Austin continued undergoing urgent care and analysis in NICU.

Austin had been close to stillborn when he was delivered, and because he was premature, they were concerned that his lungs might be underdeveloped and need support. The first report from neonatal was that Austin would require 4 weeks in the hospital as they monitored his condition. The next day, they lowered the estimate to 2 to 3 weeks. On day 3, the analysis improved to a 10-day stay; on day 4, they made it 7 days. And on day 5, our baby boy went home.

As the dismissal nurse was preparing Austin for departure, she set me up with the perfect line. "This was an unbelievable recovery. No one knew the baby was this strong!"

I responded, "Oh, yes—God knew."

She looked curiously at me, and I continued. "God told me beforehand that the baby was stronger than anyone could know."

Weeks later, I was relating the full story to my great-uncle, J. T. When I was done, he thought a moment and asked, "Isn't it amazing that God gave you comfort before you knew you needed it?"

Yes, it is amazing. God's presence was a beacon of hope that shined through our darkest moments.

God Is Forming You
Heidi Chiavaroli

I swiped at the tears wetting my cheeks and gulped back an embarrassingly vulnerable sob as I tried to gather myself in front of the women in my Wednesday night Bible study group. We had just finished a lesson on Jonah, where we were discussing Jonah's heart and actions when he blatantly disregarded God's command to go to Nineveh.

Jonah hadn't wanted to go. I secretly wondered if maybe he didn't feel spiritually strong enough.

I could relate.

I was at the end of myself. I had nowhere to turn and though I'd uttered many prayers the past two weeks, I still didn't sense God's presence. I still felt alone. Now, when our leader asked if we had any requests for prayer, I swallowed my hesitation and spoke up.

As I opened up about my struggles with strange autoimmune symptoms, the scary possibility that I would be diagnosed with lupus, hormonal imbalances, and anxiety, a tightness in my chest released. Strange, but just the act of being vulnerable—of sharing my burdens with my sisters in Christ—seemed to soften the cutting edge of my circumstances.

"I feel like Mary Magdalene with the seven demons," I confessed. "I feel like everywhere I turn, another awaits, like I can't escape." I shook my head. "I don't know, maybe I'm going crazy—I'm so up and down. I'm scared what the blood tests might reveal. I'm not sleeping well because I'm sweating through my sheets at night. I have two writing deadlines this year and I'm desperate for a way out. I'm about to search my contracts to figure out if that's even possible."

It wasn't. I'd already spent the bulk of my advances. Even if I hadn't, I was pretty sure offering to pay back my publishers to get out of my contracts was not only frowned upon, it was a career killer.

> **We also glory in our sufferings, because we know that suffering produces perseverance; perseverance, character; and character, hope.**
>
> —ROMANS 5:3–4 (NIV)

But how could I write when I could barely focus? When the passion for the projects had disappeared? Not to mention, I had another book about to release. How could I accomplish managing a launch team, planning social media posts, and responding to interviews when I could barely bring myself to open my laptop?

The woman on my left squeezed my hand, while another nodded as if she understood how I felt. They prayed for me. It reminded me of the crippled man whose friends broke through a roof to get him to Jesus. That's what these sisters were doing for me. Carrying me to Jesus.

I spoke with several of the group members after. Two of them were familiar with many of the autoimmune and hormonal battles I was going through. Maybe I wasn't as alone as I thought.

Over the next several days, though I couldn't afford to do so, I ignored my deadlines. I simply could not summon the strength to do more than go for long hikes in the woods, soak myself in Scripture, and listen to encouraging podcasts on my phone.

Then something happened. I was brushing my teeth at the sink one morning, listening to a podcast on my phone, when one sentence reached out and split me open in the best way. I looked up from spitting in the sink and stared at myself in the mirror, playing the sentence over again in my head.

"God is with you and forming you in your suffering."

I rinsed my mouth and hit the 15-second rewind on my phone twice, then listened to the sentence again. And again.

"God is with you and forming you in your suffering."

I had no idea why this statement hit me so powerfully. This was nothing I hadn't heard before. Yet I desperately needed to hear it *now*.

> **I am convinced that neither death nor life, neither angels nor demons, neither the present nor the future, nor any powers, neither height nor depth, nor anything else in all creation, will be able to separate us from the love of God that is in Christ Jesus our Lord.**
>
> —ROMANS 8:38–39 (NIV)

I realized that, until that moment, I'd viewed my suffering as simply an unfortunate thing I had to endure. I'd been faithful. I had *things* to do for God! Why was He allowing these curveballs into my life?

I'd come to think that the only suffering worthy of honoring God was suffering that involved persecution for my faith. But this one sentence from a podcast—a podcast seemingly unrelated to the topic of suffering—had wiggled its way into my spirit, planting a tiny seed of hope in my heart.

God was with me in my suffering. He could use it to draw me closer to Him.

A startling thought came to me. If a product of my suffering could be to give me *more* of Jesus, perhaps I didn't have to fear it or fight it so much. That didn't mean I should seek out suffering, but maybe I didn't need to struggle against the waves of anxiety and uncertainty as I had been. Maybe I needed to sit in my grief, and even my fear. Maybe I needed to allow Jesus to hold me in the midst of it.

> We are hard pressed on every side, but not crushed; perplexed, but not in despair; persecuted, but not abandoned; struck down, but not destroyed.
>
> —2 CORINTHIANS 4:8–9 (NIV)

As I stood in my bathroom, the peace of the Holy Spirit descended upon me. God poured out His love on me. I couldn't explain it. I could barely believe it. All I knew was that my fear melted into the tiles of my bathroom floor.

God was with me. He was really and truly with me! And wasn't that the best gift of all? No matter if I ended up with a lupus diagnosis, no matter if I couldn't make my deadlines, even if the ups-and-downs of perimenopause didn't go away eventually but stayed with me for the rest of my days, if God was with me in all of it and if these circumstances pushed me to search Him out with new fervency, then my suffering would be worth it. It wasn't a waste after all.

This truth was like a holy light switch that illuminated my core affliction and changed my perspective on my recent trials. I was able to write again. I looked at my blood tests, certain they indicated lupus, and I was not scared. With the sweet assurance of God's presence, nothing seemed too frightening, too impossible to manage. I remembered and meditated on Jesus's own suffering. I read Paul's words to the Romans and the Corinthians about hardship, committing many verses to memory so I could meditate on them during my hikes. I shared all of this with the women in my Bible study and thanked them for praying for me, certain that their prayers and their willingness to share my burden had played a role in my breakthrough.

Two weeks later, I was achieving my daily word counts, the initial passion for the contracted projects once again pushing me to meet my deadlines. My anxiety had almost dissipated, and my doctor told me my blood tests did not yet indicate a lupus diagnosis.

God in His grace had met me in this place of suffering. Even if the medical news wasn't good, even if I contracted an illness so severe that I could never write again, I'm hopeful I would have clung to Him still—maybe even clung to Him more. He *really* is the treasure.

As I look back, I realized that what I believed about God's role in the midst of my what-ifs had everything to do with how I related to my suffering. When I believed God was an impassive bystander, allowing my hurt without choosing to be intimately involved in it, I wrestled against Him and my discomfort

GOD'S GIFT OF SMELL
— Linda L. Kruschke —

WITHOUT CONSTANT WATERING with the Word of God, one's soul becomes dry and parched. The afflictions of life are difficult to bear. King David summed it up best: "You, God, are my God, earnestly I seek you; I thirst for you, my whole being longs for you, in a dry and parched land where there is no water" (Psalm 63:1, NIV). The scent of petrichor—the distinct pleasant smell of rainfall on parched earth—promises restoration and growth. To breathe it in brings hope. In the same way, God's Word brings a particular spiritual "scent" to our arid souls that promises deep refreshment and strength.

---

until it stirred up fear and anxiety. But when I was reminded of who God is—who He has proven Himself to be over and over, both in history and in my life, a God of love and compassion who genuinely cares for me and all the big and little details of my life—my hope was renewed. Nothing seems impossible with Him by my side.

God Sees in the Dark
Jeanne Takenaka

"I don't want to kill myself, but I don't want to live."

My 17-year-old son casually lobbed these words, an unexploded bomb on my heart, when we were 35,000 feet in the air.

On our way home from a summer college visit between his junior and senior years of high school, I'd been anticipating his future, and now I'd just learned that he was questioning if he had a future. I knew him well enough not to probe in that moment. But to hear that statement while storm clouds built outside our airplane window ratcheted my heart to double speed and shortened my breaths. Nearby conversations and the roar of the engine faded.

I'd learned silence was an invitation for him to speak, and my diving in with questions would only shut him down. So, I chose quiet in that moment, working to remain calm, giving him the space he needed to find words to express his thoughts. He assured me that he had no plans to take his own life. Knowing that he'd been considering the possibility was terrifying.

Our son has been good about knowing when he needed extra help to sort himself, and he'd already been meeting with his counselor for a few months. When his counselor and my husband and I noticed some changes in our son's behavior and conversation, the counselor told us that while our son was suffering from mild depression, he could still climb out of that tunnel. But a couple of weeks after my son's dramatic pronouncement on the airplane, as my husband and I sat across from our son and his counselor, the counselor confessed he'd misread the signs—that our son's depression was much more dire than he'd realized. "Death is on the table."

As our son avoided looking at my husband and me, his shoulders slumped, and my fragile ability to cope crumbled.

The beginning of his senior year of high school held no excitement for him or me. He became so withdrawn—uncommunicative and surly—that his separation felt like a divorce in our always-close relationship. His appetite declined sharply from his teen-boy norm, and eating meals together became an occasional event rather than a routine.

Worry took me captive as my son sank into the depths of depression, tunneling deeper than any of us knew he could. I opened my eyes each morning, and fear whispered, *Is this the day you wake up and he doesn't? Will you open his bedroom door and be greeted by darkness and death?*

My early morning walks in the Colorado fresh air became my safe place to cry. To beg God to help me trust Him. To pray

> **Then the angel of God called to Hagar out of heaven, and said to her, "What ails you, Hagar? Fear not, for God has heard the voice of the lad where he is. Arise, lift up the lad and hold him with your hand, for I will make him a great nation."**
>
> —GENESIS 21:17–18 (NKJV)

178 | Wrapped *in* His Protection

for His protection over our son and his mind. And, yes, to ask Him questions.

I believed that God was faithful, that He loved our children, that He loved me. But how did all of this—God's faithfulness, His love for my son, His love for me—weave together amid my son's depression and suicidal thoughts? How could I reconcile these truths with the reality that God also allows each of us free will within His sovereign plans?

I knew God was in this with me, but where was His goodness in all of this? The unknowns of God's ways in our ongoing crisis sent my thoughts into a fearful spiral and amped up my anxiety, just like those looming storm clouds outside the airplane window the day our son first confessed his struggles to me.

> The LORD appeared to us in the past, saying: "I have loved you with an everlasting love; I have drawn you with unfailing kindness."
>
> —JEREMIAH 31:3 (NIV)

I wanted to control the situation—but how does one go about controlling a teenager in the throes of depression, or the God who sees all? I grieved my son's death before he'd attempted anything. Many days, I allowed my thoughts to leap to the worst-case scenario rather than rooting them in the fact that God loved our son.

Being on the losing end of this mental battle often pushed me to belittle my own faith, which further weakened me, emotionally and physically.

God gave me trusted friends who listened to my heart. Who didn't try to fix me. Instead, they gently empathized and pointed my thoughts toward Jesus. They prayed and sent me songs to ground my heart and mind in the Lord's truths: that God gives us what we need for each day, and that God loves our son even more than my husband and I do.

One evening, while my husband, son, and I finished our supper, my husband said something he didn't know would trigger our son. Our boy fled from the table to his room and tried to stuff and control his emotions. This boy who rarely shows tears returned with red-rimmed eyes and declared the only reason he hadn't killed himself yet was because of his best friend, who seemed to be his only link to living.

> "Therefore do not worry about tomorrow, for tomorrow will worry about itself. Each day has enough trouble of its own."
>
> —MATTHEW 6:34 (NIV)

A psychologist once told me that there is a 10-minute window when a person who's been contemplating suicide will either go through with the act or back away. We'd seen our son there before, and on this night, the heat of his emotions seared us with the reality that he was in that precarious place. I listened. I prayed. We three talked until he calmed down.

About 5 weeks into our journey through darkness, I took a morning walk. Discouragement weighed me down as I begged the Lord to heal our son's depression, to protect him from himself. Unrelenting fear and anxiety had worn me out. I felt unseen by God.

While trekking a dirt trail, I glanced to the east. And stopped. A stunning sunrise layered the high clouds with vibrant oranges. The beauty of the black-eyed Susans that bordered the path swiveling their heads toward the light captivated me and filled me with God's peace. They reminded me to turn my eyes to the Light as well.

Out of curiosity, I pivoted to check out the scene to the west. In the distance, high grayish clouds hovered, and . . . A clear, vibrant rainbow arched over nearby homes, even though no rain fell.

God's words were almost audible: *I have not abandoned you, Jeanne. I see you. And I am working. Trust Me.*

Tears streamed from my eyes as I breathed in God's message. That rainbow was my reminder that I was seen, like Hagar in the desert after Abraham sent her and her son away. When she thought nobody saw her heart, when she believed she and her son would die in the desert, God spoke to her. He promised to provide for her and her son. And He did.

My Father saw and cared for me and for our son. Though I could do nothing to protect him—to heal him—my Father could.

I walked toward home, the questions that had pounded in my heart banished.

I didn't have the answers to the what-ifs that ran on repeat in my thoughts. But the One who did held me that day and in the coming weeks. It was as if He'd written a love letter in the seven colors of the rainbow, reassuring me that even though He wasn't giving me direct answers to my questions, He was bigger than our situation. And He was working on it.

Our faithful Father protected our son from himself. His counselor helped him, but more than that, God renewed his mind. In time, God drew our son out of the depths of his depression. My son once again became our exuberant teenage boy-man with a crazy appetite.

After that morning walk, I chose to trust God for the outcome—again and again. Fear that my son might die lost its grip in my thoughts and on my heart. Choosing to trust God became my protection. Like God did with Hagar and her son, God saw us in our despair and met all of our needs. He provided what we needed to walk through that dark season into the light.

Our son will probably be prone to depression for the rest of his life. He will need to make the necessary choices to remain mentally healthy. And I will choose to entrust him into my Father's hands because He's more than able to hold us through the most painful situations.

These days, whenever I see a rainbow, it's a symbol of hope when all feels hopeless—a beautiful reminder that God always sees us through every situation, no matter how dark.

A Miracle Worth Remembering
Lori Tanabe

"So, what's the story behind your tattoo?"

The question came from the woman sitting nearby me at the hotel pool.

Yes! This is what I had hoped for when I got this tattoo. I wanted it to be a conversation starter about God's work in my life.

I pulled my arm around where she could see it better. Cursive letters spelled the word "Miracle" with hearts surrounding both sides of a date: 1-31-18. "I got it after I almost died in a terrible accident. My neurosurgeon said I am a walking miracle," I told her.

I actually don't have my own memories of that fateful day, but have been able to piece together what happened through what neighbors, friends, and family have told me. And one thing is clear: God never left my side. I told the woman what I knew.

The cold January morning started like every other weekday. I was walking my two dogs before heading to work, taking the same path I always took. I was at the corner and started crossing the street when a lady in a Ford F-150 barreled into me, knocking me to the ground. My skull cracked open as I hit the pavement, and blood started pooling in the street.

Fortunately, my new neighbor, Ashley, who had moved in a month before, was coming home from dropping off her kid at school. A trained nurse, she immediately jumped out of her car, rushed to my side, and held my skull together until the ambulance arrived. Once it arrived, she rattled off directions to the EMTs on what they needed to do to keep me alive. She told me later that she had never seen so much blood in her life.

At that point, Ashley and I hadn't met, so she had no idea who I was. It was another neighbor, a teacher at a nearby school where I sometimes did substitute teaching, who passed by the bloody accident scene and shouted out, "That's Lori Tanabe!" A different neighbor tracked down my husband at his new job to let him know what had happened. I would later be thankful for their quick thinking.

> "For I know the plans I have for you," declares the LORD, "plans to prosper you and not to harm you, plans to give you hope and a future."
>
> —JEREMIAH 29:11 (NIV)

The emergency workers who responded to the call quickly determined that I needed to be airlifted to the University of Cincinnati Hospital, which specializes in head trauma cases. Fortunately, a nearby park provided the perfect place for the LifeLine helicopter to land and take off.

When I arrived at the trauma center, they put tubes in my head to try to drain the blood that was causing my brain to swell. But the swelling continued overnight, and they had to perform another surgery. They removed 6 inches of my skull, which they stored in a deep freezer for a later surgery.

That part of my skull wasn't the only thing that I lost. The accident injured my temporal lobe, which is where your nerves are connected to your senses. I completely lost my senses of smell and taste, and the doctors tell me I will never get them back. It's like they were ripped out and thrown away.

Other abilities I got back, but it was a long and painful road. After being released from the hospital, I spent months at a rehabilitation center, where I had to learn how to walk and talk again, and even how to eat again. I would put food in my mouth but didn't know what to do next; my cheeks would swell up like a chipmunk because I wasn't swallowing. The speech pathologist who was working with me on my communication also helped me learn how to swallow and eat again.

> Give thanks in all circumstances; for this is God's will for you in Christ Jesus.
>
> —1 THESSALONIANS 5:18 (NIV)

As I spent Easter in rehab, my physical therapists arranged for an Easter egg hunt for me. Every time I opened up an egg, there were directions for a rehab exercise that I had to perform in front of them. They were so excited about the creativity of the game, but I hated it.

Six weeks after that Easter egg hunt, I had a third and final surgery to put my skull back together. I was very fortunate to be under the care of an experienced and gifted neurosurgeon. Not only was he a renowned surgeon, but he was also a caring, personable caregiver who joked, when I asked him how many surgeries like this he had performed, "Oh, I've done a couple."

Throughout the whole ordeal, my local community and church were such amazing support, not only for me but my whole family. My daughter, Jayleigh, set up a GoFundMe account to raise money for hospital expenses, and other friends and acquaintances organized fundraisers also. A friend set up Meal Trains for my family. Pastors from my church visited me.

A friend of mine who attended a different church held a prayer vigil for me at the park while I was in intensive care. Over 100 people came for it, including a young girl I worked with at my part-time job at Walgreens. When I went back to work months later, she told me that it was through attending the prayer vigil that she started going back to church. Her mom joined her soon after. A year later, she was baptized at my home church, attributing her faith in God to the miracles she witnessed through my accident.

My own faith was bolstered when I saw God provide for my family in special ways. The accident brought family members like my cousin and sister, who had been at odds with each other, back together again. And a year after the accident, I went to visit my mom in California to show her that I was physically fine. I attended church service with her and asked if I could speak to her Sunday school class of nearly sixty people. I wanted to thank them for all their prayers and for being by my mom's side.

When I went back to work as a substitute teacher the following school year, I found out how my accident had impacted the teachers and students. On the day of the accident, they heard the helicopter. My teacher friends told me it was the worst day ever and they couldn't stop crying. Shortly after the accident, two elementary-age boys set up a big poster in the cafeteria and people signed it. Later they brought the poster to my room at the rehab facility. On my first day back to school, the students screamed and cried, and some almost knocked me down from their excitement.

People showed their support in little ways, too. The long, black, curly hair that I had before the accident had to be shaved off for surgery. The first time I saw myself in the mirror I cried; later, I joked that I was just going to paint my head purple. The next day one of the hospital workers brought me a purple wig, and it boosted my mood. While my hair grew out, which took close to a year, Jayleigh would bring me wigs to wear, and a cousin sent me a wig with blonde hair that was longer than mine had ever been. I called it my "mermaid" wig. When I went back to my job at Walgreens, the other workers would try to guess what color wig I would show up in that day.

It took me a while to get over my bitterness toward the lady who hit me. It wasn't only the long, painful recovery. My body is weaker than it was before, and I'm sore most days, although I push through it. I have a dent in my head and still suffer odd head pains that are different from the headaches I used to have before the accident. Most of all, I miss being able to taste and smell. But whenever I lamented my lost senses, my daughter would always remind me, "Mom, you lost the best senses you could lose. You didn't lose your life. You're not blind; you can see."

> **My times are in your hands; deliver me from the hands of my enemies, from those who pursue me.**
>
> —PSALM 31:15 (NIV)

God's miracles throughout this traumatic time are documented in a journal that Jayleigh put together during my weeks in the hospital and rehab. In one entry, she wrote, "Dear Mom, it's been over a year since the accident and you are doing amazing! No one can get over how miraculous your recovery was!"

Now, I told my new friend at the pool, "You know, I almost didn't get the tattoo." I was too scared to get one, so I penned a temporary one with a body marker. "My daughter has always joked about how I'd survived three brain surgeries but was scared to get a little tattoo."

One day I joined my daughter at her own tattoo appointment and finally felt it was time to make my temporary tattoo permanent. As I began telling her tattoo artist the story behind my "Miracle" tattoo, he stopped me and said, "Wait right here." He left and brought out another artist, who said he needed to show me something. He pulled out his ID from his wallet and showed me that his last name was Miracle.

"That's your sign, Mom," Jayleigh said. So I booked my appointment with Mr. Miracle and made my tattoo permanent.

I will never forget the amazing ways that God held me in His hands through my tragic ordeal. I only have to look down at my arm to be reminded of His goodness!

Grace for the Long Haul
Carolyn Waverly

December 26. Remnants of gold ribbons and opened presents were scattered under the tree. Our daughter, home for the holidays, was still in bed when we left for the doctor's office.

The nurse had called me a few days earlier. "The doctor needs you to come with your husband to his appointment on the 26th." Her words hovered over me through Christmas Day. Will had recently finished a series of tests. *Are we facing hard news?*

The doctor sat down with us. "There's no easy way to say this, so I'll just say it: You have the Alzheimer's type of dementia." We managed to ask a couple of questions, then sought refuge in our SUV, where we held each other and sobbed.

In my heart, I had feared this news. The previous 6 months had planted questions in my mind. Questions that I didn't share with anyone. Misplacing his driver's license and credit card and cell phone. Lacking any interest in the stack of books by his chair. Telling lengthy stories about playing football in high school and college while our dear friends patiently listened. Putting mouthwash and Band-Aids he just bought in the fridge. And snipping at me. Looking at the menu at a restaurant, he sounded defeated. "I don't know what to order. There are too many choices." *Is this a normal part of aging?* My mind jumped to other areas of his life. *If this continues, how can he do his job?*

When his secretary raised questions about him, I took a few days to pray. Over brunch after church, I pleaded with him to retire. When he nodded and teared up, I asked, "Is it OK for me to call your doctor for an appointment?"

Parallel to those same six-plus months, entries from my journal read: July 28, after he was so agitated for forgetting his order in the drive-thru lane: "This used to be my journal. Now it's my friend. The questions. The pain. The record of our lives." September 24, after scheduling all these appointments with doctors, neurological testing, and MRI—during the holidays, and before he retired at year's end: "It's so hard! I feel overwhelmed! Gratefully, God doesn't change—His Sovereignty, His love, mercy, and grace." November 9, when he told me not to tell anyone what was going on, and I didn't. "I am stressed! But I want to write all this down so I can look back and see how the Lord held my hand. Praying for wisdom."

The diagnosis on that day after Christmas offered us a name for the change that would overtake our lives. His unwanted retirement in the cloudy, cold, and icy month of January set the stage for the perfect season to grieve. We apologized more to each other that winter than in our previous 40 years of marriage. Tempted to just stay in bed many mornings, I got up when I heard the shower. If he could power through, couldn't

> Trust in the LORD with all your heart and lean not on your own understanding; in all your ways submit to him, and he will make your paths straight.
>
> —PROVERBS 3:5–6 (NIV)

I? Thankfully, our two preschool grandchildren spent a day with us every week, and we mustered up enough perk for them. We're both organizers and planners. This was *not* our plan! I had just rebounded from being my mom's caregiver for a decade. *I can't do this again, God!*

We love to tell the story of the improbability that the two of us would ever meet. How would a high school English teacher and an engineer come into contact through our work when we lived 90 minutes apart? It happened through an annual dinner where our jobs intersected. Several of my students were essay contest finalists. His boss needed him to fill in as tour director for the company-sponsored, all-expense-paid trip to Washington, DC. As their teacher, I was invited to the award dinner for the winners. A few months went by before he tried to reach out to me. Knowing only my name and where I worked—this was the 1980s, before social media and Google—he wrote me a letter and mailed it to the high school.

> **Those who know your name trust in you, for you, LORD, have never forsaken those who seek you.**
>
> —PSALM 9:10 (NIV)

Both of us grew up on third-generation family farms and graduated from high school the same year. His sister and I shared the same name. Our upbringing had more similarities than differences. Our families even had the same picture of

Jesus on the walls of our houses. Bruised and broken from divorces, we ever-so-slowly spilled out our hearts to each other. One story at a time. Wanting to start over, he had taken a job 700 miles and three states away. "You'll meet a girl from Illinois and never move back," his dad told him. But could he trust again? Could I? Three years, endless miles, and one speeding ticket later, we walked down the aisle on a warm, windy October Saturday. God brought us together as such an abundant gift of grace.

The same question kept coming to my mind, an epiphany of sorts. An eternal whisper. I woke at three in the morning to those same four words. *Do you trust Me?* I knew they came from above.

I've struggled with fear and worry much of my life. Did I trust Him when Will went into a commission-only job, and we didn't have enough money for the house payment one month, then another? Did I trust Him when our daughter was the victim of a serious crime? Did I trust Him when my husband had a heart bypass in his fifties? Did I trust Him when my dad got colon cancer? Did I trust Him with the difficulty of caregiving for Mom? And now, did I trust Him with my husband's Alzheimer's? Looking back on my timeline, God has been there above it celebrating with me. And below, in the valleys, His arms surrounding me. I mourn what we've lost and still have moments of anticipatory grief, but I don't camp out there. His goodness and grace are never beyond my reach.

I called Will my personal trainer. We'd be sitting in our matching leather chairs after dinner, and he would announce, "When do you want to leave to go to the Y?" I would drag myself out of the chair, and he would set my weights for me when we got to the gym. Now I initiate. "Let's go for a walk."

He kept up on all things newsworthy current events: global, White House, our state capital, and local. I needed to as well, because I knew Will would want to talk about what was going on. Who would have thought someday I'd miss that? Now we discuss the news in small bites.

Travel brochures and travelogues are shelved in his office, waiting for the different post-retirement life we'd anticipated. Now we travel only to places we've visited before. My counselor's suggestion. We've exchanged adventure for comfort. And who doesn't like comfort? Like a faded sweatshirt or the favorite shoes that were broken in too many seasons ago.

For years he talked about having his own home office, describing it in detail. We used to share one, but finally I cleaned out an extra bedroom. We brought up the cherry wood bookshelves stored in the basement, and he filled the shelves with his plethora of books and framed family pictures. He picked out a beautiful matching desk and hung favorite pictures from his work office. With the glory of the morning sun pouring through the double windows, he now sits at his desk. His Bible spread open. In his sanctuary. He is content, as am I.

> So we praise God for the glorious grace he has poured out on us who belong to his dear Son.
>
> —EPHESIANS 1:6 (NIV)

Recently, I walked by an end cap of cards at the grocery store. One caught my eye. A cross on the front with the words "God is good." I needed a reminder that day. The inside read: "And hope is reborn. Moment by moment." *Who buys herself a card?* Me. It sits on the windowsill above my kitchen sink. We have far more good moments than hard ones.

The "no longer" list grows, but we're beyond grateful for the "still cans." He is Pops to our preschool grandchildren. Running through the sprinkler. Raking leaf piles to jump in. Pushing their swing under the tree. Shooting hoops. Endlessly pitching a ball to a boy who endlessly wants to hit it. Planting and tending to their strawberries and tomatoes. Doing simple puzzles. Reading books to them. Trying different ice cream shops. Cheering at ball games.

Illinois weather offers four distinct seasons. Alzheimer's has three: spring, summer, and fall. We have navigated its spring and summer—the "quirky" stage, I called it. But now we need a jacket. There's a nip in the air. Recently, the doctor suggested a new medication for the chillier days ahead.

This isn't the retirement life we envisioned. It's simpler, slower, and more sacred. *Do I trust Him? How can I not?*

Hope for the Future
Mindy Baker

My son's senior year of high school caused me many anxious days and sleepless nights. When my children were toddlers and elementary aged, I felt I was more in charge of things. There were outside influences that I feared, but I was able to set clear boundaries of protection and made it a priority to spend quality time with them in order to teach them about the Lord and His ways. During their high school years, my role shifted significantly, and I felt the weight of it. I was still my son's mom, but now my role was more of a coach. Even though my intention was to help and support him, it seemed like all I did was nag and irritate him. As my son began to spread his wings more and more with each passing day, I felt tormented by worry and helplessly out of control.

Selecting a college was a huge ordeal. First came countless college visits, all of them more awkward than the next. I felt my emotional distance from my son more than ever as it seemed like I couldn't do anything right. My only solace was that at each visit, when I glanced around the room filled with other students my son's age they were equally embarrassed by their parents. All of us were trying to navigate the uncomfortableness of it all.

Next came the college applications. It was a lengthy process that was not for the faint of heart. Feeling the pressure to make sure my son didn't miss an opportunity, I micromanaged every step of the process, and it seemed as if I had to constantly needle and coax him to complete the next task. The more I pushed, the more he shut down. I was beyond frustrated. Part of me understood that I should let go and allow him the freedom to take care of the details on his own, but for some reason I couldn't.

During his junior year and most of his senior year, my son was set on informatics (the study of how we process information and how we can use technology to help visualize it) as his career path, so at every college visit we always inquired about that major. However, in his senior year, he participated in a computer programming internship at a local business that he didn't enjoy at all. At the same time, he was discovering a love of filmmaking, and he was considering changing his major. The problem? He had been awarded a significant scholarship from a state school based on his intention to enroll as an informatics major. The money was tied to that major. He could do a double-major with film and keep the money, but if he opted to do only the film major, he would lose that scholarship. It all seemed foggy and confusing. *Why wasn't God's plan clearer?*

> **Yes, my soul, find rest in God; my hope comes from him.**
>
> —PSALM 62:5 (NIV)

While my son was debating, my husband, on a whim, had the idea of touring a Christian college that was located many hours from our house. He and my son booked a weekend trip to visit the college. They had a great experience and loved the film program, but my son still wasn't convinced enough to make a decision. Time was ticking, and I wanted him to decide. But this was a decision I could not make for him.

GOD'S GIFT OF HEARING
— Linda L. Kruschke —

GOD, THE GRAND creator of all things, said to the ocean, "This far you may come and no farther; here is where your proud waves halt" (Job 38:11, NIV). The waves of the ocean crash loudly upon the shores of every continent. Standing on a busy beach and listening to that unceasing sound, one can sense the power of God, who holds back the waters of the deep. The waves may roar in protest or quietly lap the sandy shore in submission to the Almighty. Each Christian faces the same choice: to protest or to obey. What is the sound that *your* spirit makes?

As the stress continued to mount, I often read Scripture aloud as a practical way to calm my heart. I remember one sleepless night when my worry came to a breaking point. In my living room I got down on my knees and prayed. *I acknowledge that You are in control, Lord. I trust in Your plan for his life.* After I finished praying, I felt a release in my spirit and a peace washed over me. I was finally accepting the truth: I was never in control at all; only God was. As much as I loved my son, God loved him infinitely more. He had a perfect plan for my son's future. After that encounter, I slept soundly. God showed me that He was perfectly capable of directing my son, and that I needed to get out of the way.

Eventually, like all difficult decisions, my son wrestled through it and made his choice: he would major in film at the university he and my husband had visited months previously.

Once he told us his decision, I again felt peace. I knew it was the right decision, and I praised God for leading him in spite of all of my control issues. Even though I didn't have all the answers about what the future would hold, I felt free.

The day we dropped him off and said good-bye, tears streamed down my face. First, my heart was full as I recognized and experienced the wonderful privilege of watching God's plan for my son's life unfold. But I was also filled with emotion as I realized how God had used His Word over the previous months to calm my restless heart and remind me that I can find supernatural rest and hope in Him alone. He is trustworthy. He is faithful. And He has not only me wrapped in His protection, but also my children.

Reassurance During a Time of Silence

Barbara Latta

"The Twin Towers have fallen, and the Pentagon has been bombed," the church secretary announced to my women's Bible study group.

What?

The friendly banter we had enjoyed only moments before ceased. A room full of women sat in shock for a few moments trying to absorb the message we had just heard.

I didn't wait around for more information, if there was any. I grabbed my Bible and notebook and ran toward the church exit. The rush to find my keys caused my Bible, purse, and all its contents to spew onto the parking lot.

"No, I don't need this now," I fussed under my breath as I gathered my possessions—along with a lot of dirt—and threw them into the car. It took my shaking hands multiple tries to insert the key into the ignition. I couldn't get home fast enough; I don't know how I didn't get a speeding ticket.

September 11, 2001, is a date we will never forget. The unspeakable events caught our nation by surprise. And for members of the military like my husband, Ken, it would mean dramatic changes in the scope and nature of their service.

Ken, a Naval reservist, was serving on active-duty orders in Saudi Arabia during this time. Yes, a Navy guy in the middle of sand with no water in sight.

Ken served in this branch of the military for several years in the mid-eighties, then, due to job relocations, didn't rejoin when his enlistment time ended. Where we were living, he wouldn't have been able to fulfill the requirements of a reservist.

In 1998, that all changed. He loved the military and, because we had moved to a city close to Atlanta, he had more opportunities to train and serve on the monthly drill weekends.

After weeks of specialized instruction to be an intelligence analyst, he received an offer to go to Saudi Arabia. Even though his training was over, he still had to wait on the security clearances his job would require. This usually takes months and sometimes over a year, but his came through in less than a month.

This was a miracle in itself. This told us God wanted him to take this assignment and that He was the one who had placed Ken in that position.

In 2001, Ken and I didn't have cell phones. Although we had a landline in our home, once he went overseas, he didn't have regular access to a phone to call me, so our only communication was through email. On the fateful day of 9/11, the first thing I did after arriving at home was turn on the computer and check for a message from him. Nothing I saw gave me the connection I needed.

I turned on the TV, and the images left me stunned. This was not a Hollywood movie. This was a tragedy happening in real time. An airliner plunged into a building and disappeared in seconds in a sea of flames. Concrete and steel crumbled followed by waves of smoke and ash.

How and why did this happen?

At the time of this event, no one knew the cause of this tragedy. My mind raced with imagined scenarios. I reasoned if the Pentagon had been bombed, military bases may have been too. Ken was 8,000 miles away. What was happening over there?

I paced. I prayed. I called friends to pray for him.

Our oldest son was in the Army and stationed in Korea. Our youngest was still in high school, but even that afternoon when he came home from school and in the days that followed, our individual fears and worry prevented us from comforting each other. Our other family members lived in faraway states. I couldn't run to my mother and cry on her shoulder.

I waited hourly for the ding that indicated an email in the inbox. Each time the sound rang out, I jumped to the computer and clicked to open the message. But there was only junk mail. Days went by with nothing but a cluttered inbox with ads and messages I didn't want to read.

> "The LORD himself goes before you and will be with you; he will never leave you nor forsake you. Do not be afraid; do not be discouraged."
>
> —DEUTERONOMY 31:8 (NIV)

Surely if the compound where he worked had been hit in some way, I would have heard by now, wouldn't I?

Another email notification alerted me. Kind friends asking for news.

"Have you heard from Ken?"

"Are you all right?"

Wrapped in His Protection

Ken's parents and siblings called asking the same questions. I had no news for them either.

I read my Bible and prayed but the words blurred through my tears. The messages didn't penetrate the fear in my mind. Sleep evaded me. Each time I closed my eyes the fiery images I had viewed jerked me into what-if scenarios.

"God, I'm so scared. What is happening in our country? What is happening in the world? I know You tell us not to be afraid, but I feel so alone."

I'm here.

The words I heard in my heart caused me to stop and listen. I had been so overcome by fear, God's voice had been blocked out.

The next day an email from a precious Christian friend shared scriptures of hope that I clung to as my life preserver. Among these were Psalm 27:3 (NIV), "Though an army besiege me, my heart will not fear; though war break out against me, even then I will be confident."

> **Let us then approach God's throne of grace with confidence, so that we may receive mercy and find grace to help us in our time of need.**
>
> —HEBREWS 4:16 (NIV)

These words reminded me that God was there and always had been.

Each time talons of fear tried to dig into my thoughts, I read these verses again. I realized this is where I should have been from day one. Peace surrounded me and that night my eyes closed in slumber for the first time in days.

The scriptures from my friend became my strength over the days ahead and reminded me that God is always with us. Just because I couldn't feel Him didn't mean He wasn't there. His ever-present hand was with me. Each time I worried, His Word was my reassurance during this time of silence from overseas.

After seven long days with no news, the message I longed for brought relief and joy. An email from Ken. He assured me he was OK and all was well in their location. The lapse in contact was due to officials freezing all communications into and out of the country for security reasons.

Weeks later, sources shared with me that the 9/11 terrorists originated in Saudi Arabia. Had I known this from the beginning, my fear would have escalated. But God knew exactly the information I needed. The delay in hearing from Ken was an opportunity for me to grow my faith in the Lord.

The events of this tragic day changed Ken's orders and delayed his homecoming. But he did eventually return safely, and I couldn't thank God enough.

Future assignments in the fight against terrorism sent him back to the Middle East. But my worries dissipated under the shadow of the Almighty as I held on to the same words that sustained me during Ken's first overseas tour of duty.

The Lord still reminds me daily that He is my refuge and strength.

I know that I've been guided by God. I am obedient.

—Maya Angelou

CHAPTER 5

Guided to Safety

A Secondhand Sweater and Two Mangoes 206
    Ingrid Skarstad

Graced with a Concussion. 212
    Kerry Duprez, as told to Claire McGarry

Is God on Vacation? 219
    Amanda Pennock

. . . But God 223
    Kelly Farley

In the Crosshairs. 230
    Diana DeSpain Schramer

Healing Hands 236
    Kathlyn C. White

A Secondhand Sweater and Two Mangoes
Ingrid Skarstad

"Wake up, Ingrid!" The shout was my own. I pounded the steering wheel in time to the music, shook my head, then slapped my face to keep my eyes from closing.

Why am I so tired? I felt myself dozing off again and shouted, "God, please help me!"

This 14-hour drive was not new, but it became frequent after my father's health soured. If I needed a nap, I stayed close to the interstate and snoozed in a well-lit, busy gas station or truck stop. If I needed real sleep, I had favorite locations to stay overnight—except along this portion, a significant new detour.

The combination of the unfamiliar road and the long drive made me unusually tired, and I was afraid if I kept going I'd fall asleep at the wheel. I pulled over and looked at my hotel app. There was nothing near me, only in cities along the interstate I just left. I knew I couldn't make it that far. I asked Google to find hotels near me. There was only one. I called.

A woman with a strong accent answered the phone and reluctantly agreed to host me. It seemed that a single woman traveling through the lone prairie was suspicious somehow! I was too weary to reassure her.

Two highways later, I entered the tiny town and raised my eyebrows as I rolled toward the hotel. It looked less desirable than I expected. *What have I done?* I kept rolling.

I drove through to get the lay of the land, which wasn't much. My round trip to the grain elevators at the edge of town couldn't have been more than four blocks, but it included a circular memorial built into a modern roundabout—statues, flags, benches, and a circular sidewalk. It was like a roundabout within a roundabout! I noticed a restaurant next to the hotel as I returned. My stomach growled. My eyes drooped. *I might as well stay.* Intoxicating tiredness still had me in its grip.

> **"Your Father knows what you need before you ask Him."**
>
> —MATTHEW 6:8 (AMPC)

The hotel appeared as if it had been renovated from two or three slightly dilapidated buildings. Under the Vacancy sign sat a small Nativity scene—a plastic Mary and Joseph gazing lovingly into what should have been a manger. It was a terracotta planter that had been used as an ash tray.

There was no lobby. Well, there *was* an area that could receive guests, but it seemed unused for that purpose, and it was locked. Papers stuffed behind the counter peeked out through the window. The woman had told me to call when I arrived, so I did.

A short, dark-haired woman came to the door and half-shouted through the panes, "Come to the room!" and pointed to the left.

I found an unmarked door in that direction and stepped into a dark, paneled hallway. Handwritten signs sprinkled the walls, which were painted purple above the paneling. Carpets ribbed with years of use covered the walkway. The woman was not there, but there was only one way to go, so I followed it until I turned a corner and saw an open door.

The woman bustled about the room checking for supplies and smoothing the wrinkles on the beds. "I put the television on for you so you can keep up with the storm." She handed a form to me and asked for payment.

I fished in my purse and asked, "Storm?"

"Oh yes. It is coming!" She paused while I filled out paperwork. My stomach must have growled again. "If you need to eat, go to the restaurant next door right now. They close in bad weather."

Bad weather? Storm? I didn't see signs of either. I also didn't see a grocery store in town, which is my usual go-to when I stay anywhere. I didn't have much packed for snacks, so I set out after she handed me the key. The woman pointed down the long hall, urged me to lock my door—something about too many people coming in—and disappeared.

Too many people coming in? Maybe I should have kept driving!

The front of the restaurant held a few tables and booths flocked in red-and-white checkerboard patterns. A large Closed sign stood just inside the door. The place was empty, but the outer door was unlocked, so I stepped in.

"Hello?"

A waitress peeked out from a wide opening at the back of the room. Her eyes had a hurried look, as if I had distracted her from something important.

I asked, "May I order food to go?"

"Possibly." She waved me in.

I followed her through the back hallway that led to an arcade, bowling alley, and finally a bar with a small dance floor. Three people bustled around the cash register, two girls donned coats, and one looked for an umbrella.

The young man was in charge. "Sure, I'd be glad to whip up something for you. First, I've got to get these girls out so they can beat the storm." He slid a menu across the wooden bar while the girls signed out.

"Reuben sandwich," I said, and slid the menu back.

As I waited on the impromptu cook, I looked through the window to find some sign of a storm. Nothing. But everyone seemed to be in a hurry! The weather seemed pleasant to me, so I targeted a bench in the miniature memorial park, which was directly across the street, and took my meal there as the employees cleared out.

> **Casting the whole of your care . . . on Him, for He cares for you affectionately and cares about you watchfully.**
>
> —1 PETER 5:7 (AMPC)

I nestled into a seat with a view of the flags against the cloudy sky. It was slightly gray, but the air was comfortable, and the town was as still as a picture book. I relaxed, thankful to have a place to eat and rest. *Another adventure*, I mused. *I'll probably write about this one.*

Dark clouds moved in behind the flags. Raindrops arrived with a "ta-da!" and danced on my food. I scrambled back into the dark hotel and sat on the bed to eat the rest of my perfectly greasy Reuben sandwich.

The news was still on. Tornadoes. Hail. High winds. Somber meterologists telling people to take cover. Evidently the weather wasn't just "bad" but dangerous! The television signal came and went with pixelated pauses and reconnections until the signal was lost completely.

Wind began to blow, and in moments, extreme weather swept in. I prayed for my car on the unprotected sidewalk. I prayed for the hotel. I prayed for the businesses and families in the tiny town. I spoke to the storm like Jesus did, "Peace! Be still!"

Wind died down. Rain continued. And I went to sleep.

When I woke and all appeared well, I thanked God for His protection through the night.

I ignored the shower and brought my keys outside to the depository near the "office" door. I intended to rise early and leave so I could make up for lost time and get to my dad's place by early evening—maybe even get there in time to catch the sunset over the small lake. But on my way out to the car, I was tempted to stop and take pictures of the nativity.

The owner hustled outside, and I immediately felt guilty. "Is this OK? I was just taking photos for myself."

She didn't answer directly. "Come. Come. I make coffee for you."

Watered-down coffee turned into breakfast.

Breakfast turned into a hotel tour.

The tour turned into lounging in her cluttered living quarters.

We became friends in those morning hours.

Lynn (not her real name) became a Christian in Egypt at the cost of being ejected from her family. She cannot go back. But as long as she stays in the United States, she is free to believe and worship Jesus. In her living room there is a large image of His face painted on velvet and framed in plastic. She adored it.

She has not fully escaped persecution, however. Her tiny town has some people who do not understand. They ridicule her (and I witnessed it at the gas station by the highway when I left). Yet joy and generosity still rise in her, and she continues to offer gifts to them during Christmas to celebrate Jesus.

I helped her clean my room. I saw the other side of the hotel with the renovations she had done. We snacked on mangoes while she shared worship videos with me in her language and translated the lyrics for me. The music moved her, and her love for the Lord moved me.

"I have something for you!" Lynn rummaged through clothing stacked on top of her dog crates. She held out a black sweater with sparkles of silver woven throughout. "I like this for you. We are friends, yes?"

"Yes, we are friends."

We talked about writing her story one day. She gave me her phone number, hugs, and when I declined staying for lunch, urged me to take two mangoes for the road.

I accepted and went on my way—concerned about the time I spent but thrilled with the morning adventure.

When I reached the original interstate I left for the detour, I noticed effects of the storm for hundreds of miles as I drove: mangled billboards, felled trees, abandoned vehicles in ditches. It all happened on a long stretch of road through sparse states where I would have driven the night before.

Wow! Did God ever help me!

No wonder the unusual sleepiness wouldn't leave me the day before! I thought I needed to wake up and drive, but God knew I needed to get out of the storm and stay alive—and maybe make a new friend in the process.

Graced with a Concussion

Kerry Duprez, as told to Claire McGarry

"Just go and get checked out," I said to my husband, Kurt, after his boss, Jason, suggested he might have a concussion.

While at his job at the firehouse the night before, Kurt had bumped his head on the corner of the wall-mounted TV. Despite experiencing a headache, dizziness, and nausea, he still went to his other job the next day, where he worked with Jason doing small-engine repairs.

As a fireman of 32 years, Kurt got injured a lot. It was part of the job. In fact, he'd had five major injuries in the past 6 years, four of which had resulted in surgeries. Despite that—or maybe because of it—he'd learned to take it all in stride, and was prone to shrugging things off. But as a former paramedic, Jason knew a thing or two about head trauma. He wouldn't let up on Kurt until he agreed to go to urgent care.

I'd just been there 4 days before with our daughter, Mahre. She'd bumped her head on a low-hanging pipe in the woodworking shop at school. I presumed the process would be the same: Kurt would get checked out and be told all was fine, just like they'd told Mahre.

When the phone rang later, Kurt's first words were, "Kerry, they found something."

With my typical sarcasm, I responded, "Great! They did find a brain."

Kurt didn't play along with our usual banter. What he told me instead obliterated my bubble of humor, wrapping my heart in a vice-grip of fear.

Urgent Care had referred Kurt to the emergency room for a CT scan, which revealed swelling in the ventricles of his brain. More shockingly, the follow-up MRI revealed a tumor attached to his cerebellum, blocking 95 percent of the cerebrospinal fluid going to and from his brain. None of this had anything to do with the bump he got at the firehouse. It was what they call an "incidental finding," where one injury leads to the discovery of a completely unrelated problem.

On the Uber ride to the hospital, my thoughts spun out of control. Was the tumor cancerous? Would Kurt die? What about all the things we still wanted to do together? What about that trip to Italy we always promised each other?

That's when I texted my mom and sisters requesting prayers for Kurt, of course, but also for myself. Kurt had always been the rock in our family. I was the emotional one who cried during sappy commercials. With our lives about to be thrown into the complete unknown, I knew one thing for certain: I had to be the strong one for Kurt and our four young-adult children.

Having seen the incredible impact of prayer on the lives of others, and even on my own, I believed in prayer wholeheartedly.

> **So do not fear, for I am with you; do not be dismayed, for I am your God. I will strengthen you and help you; I will uphold you with my righteous right hand.**
>
> —ISAIAH 41:10 (NIV)

But until that crisis, I had never *felt* its power. As my mom's and sisters' prayers went up to heaven, I became a different person. Rather than being overwhelmed by fear, peace descended as I sat beside Kurt in his hospital room watching doctors do one neurological test after another. Rather than my thoughts getting scattered as medical team after medical team paraded through the room, each giving their own interpretation of the situation, I became laser focused: taking notes, asking clarifying questions, and making sure Kurt was getting what he needed. It was a phenomenon I struggle to define in words, even today. The closest I can come is to say I felt held up by a presence that was real, by my side the entire time, and truly tangible.

Even when the doctors started talking about emergency brain surgery within a matter of hours, I never once let a tear fall. Instead, I was able to reassure Kurt and my kids with a confidence I truly felt. What was concerning was that the surgeon at the local hospital where we were had never performed surgery on this type of tumor before. Subependymomas—slow-growing, benign brain tumors—are so rare that even the top brain surgeon in our region had done less than ten operations to remove one in his entire 22-year career. Because the tumor was attached to the top of Kurt's spinal cord, one wrong move could leave him incapacitated for the rest of his life. Or, worse yet, end his life.

By the grace of God, the doctors agreed that surgery could wait while we got everything in order. Of course, what we wanted most was to get that top surgeon in our area, who worked out of Massachusetts General Hospital, to be the one who operated on Kurt. Boston was only 20 minutes away, after all. But there were people from all over the world trying to be seen at that hospital and by that surgeon. The odds of us getting in were slim to none.

God continued to respond to the barrage of prayers being said on our behalf, placing people in our path to guide us. "So-and-so knows so-and-so, who happens to know that surgeon," said the chain of texts from family and friends. That breadcrumb trail of messages is how we miraculously found ourselves in the office of that top surgeon at Massachusetts General Hospital within days. However, we quickly found out that just getting an appointment with him wasn't enough. It was hard to hear him say that he had a long list of patients waiting for surgery, and "one brain tumor doesn't take priority over another." Still, we hung on to hope and that tangible feeling that God was with us, working on our behalf. That was confirmed when we got the phone call a few days later saying that there was a cancellation with that surgeon, and they could fit Kurt in!

> I will instruct you and teach you in the way you should go; I will counsel you with my loving eye on you.
>
> —PSALM 32:8 (NIV)

There were times, of course, when despair tried to creep in. It happened most during the endless phone calls with the insurance company trying to get approval for surgery at Mass General. They were willing to foot the bill at our local hospital, with the inexperienced surgeon, but that is where they drew the line. I only broke down and cried twice during the entire crisis. Each time was on one of those phone calls when I was explaining what could happen to Kurt if the inexperienced surgeon made one wrong move. As I painted the picture of my husband being unable to walk, talk, swallow, see, or even hug our kids, reality crashed in. As embarrassed as I was about sobbing on the phone to two different total strangers, it seemed that was part of God's plan too. Apparently, my description of my husband as a complete invalid, and my heartfelt tears, touched their hearts, inspiring each one to sign off on her step of the process, moving the application along.

Nevertheless, we were still in insurance-coverage limbo right up until the day before the surgery. The operation was only the tip of the financial iceberg. Post-op, Kurt would have to go to the neurological intensive care unit so he could be monitored 24/7 for any buildup of pressure in his brain. He was already working two jobs to pay our expenses before this all happened. How would we ever recover financially if we had to foot this $174,000 bill too?

Then the phone rang. It was the final decision-maker in the very lengthy chain of insurance red tape. She called to say that the *only* reason she was approving our application was because of the two women I'd cried to before. She called each one an "expert in her field." She also explained that that was why she was so upset because, in her words, "they each made the mistake" of moving the application along. All I could think was that those two women were more than experts—they were angels who had followed God's promptings, playing their part in the miracle He was orchestrating.

The next day, exactly two weeks from when Kurt first went to the ER, he was wheeled into the operating room of one of the top five hospitals in the world to be operated on by one of the most experienced surgeons in the country. That statement alone was concrete evidence of God's hand at work. But I know His intervention hadn't stopped there.

Prior to this, I had always known that God was trustworthy, but I had battled with placing my full trust in His hands. What if His will for me was different from what I wanted for myself? I knew He used hardships for our good, but I'm only human. I didn't want to invite those hardships in. So, I continued to hold certain circumstances tight, praying to God to change them for the better, but unwilling to surrender fully to Him in case He willed a different outcome.

Yet, hour after hour, as I sat in the waiting room of that hospital while the surgeon slowly trimmed away one layer after another of my husband's brain tumor, I realized God had been doing the same thing with my heart: peeling away one layer after another of resistance, doubt, and fear. I discovered I was now 100 percent willing to accept His will for us. If Kurt died on that operating table, I trusted God to carry us through. If Kurt ended up completely incapacitated, God would equip me to care for him. There wasn't a single scenario I could come up with that filled me with dread or fear. God was in control. I believed wholeheartedly that His will would be for our good, no matter what that looked like to me. He'd faithfully carried us through this far. He'd continue to do so, no matter what. That realization flooded my soul with a peace that cannot be described, but one I wish I could bottle and give to the world.

> **I will be glad and rejoice in your love, for you saw my affliction and knew the anguish of my soul.**
>
> —PSALM 31:7 (NIV)

When the surgeon finally came to the waiting room to tell us the results of the operation, the pensive look on his face had

GOD'S GIFT OF TOUCH
— Terrie Todd —

A TODDLER WHO knows that a stove is hot will avoid it even when it's cold, especially if that lesson was learned the hard way—with a burned hand. God's gift of touch (nerve endings that send messages to the brain) causes us to pull away from a hot surface, avoiding worse damage. Because leprosy kills those nerve endings, lepers can suffer from injuries that they didn't feel, and therefore didn't prevent. In this practical sense, even pain is a gift from God, though we rarely value it. We can also appreciate what a deep life healing Jesus gave to lepers when He healed them of their affliction.

---

me thinking, *This isn't going to be good.* I was so worried it took me a moment to fully comprehend his words when he told us that the surgery was a success. Kurt would be fine!

To this day, I still don't know why that surgeon had such a pensive look on his face when his message was so positive. I suppose it's just one more reminder that things are never how they appear on the surface. Even the most horrific experiences carry gifts in their hands. The gift I received was being transformed from a person who always lived in fear of the worst-case scenario to being completely surrendered to God's plan, no matter the outcome.

The outcome for Kurt was the successful removal of a brain tumor and the steady journey back to good health. The outcome for me was the true and complete conversion of my heart.

Is God on Vacation?
Amanda Pennock

It had been the hardest year of my life. My marriage of almost 40 years was falling apart. I had started drinking a lot of alcohol to help numb my pain, which only made things worse. Finally, I realized that I was powerless over alcohol and was recommended to a twelve-step program. In this program, I felt right at home and made new friends. I was told to get a sponsor, someone who has gone through the twelve steps and would help me go through them. I chose a woman who was at every meeting and had been in the program for over 25 years.

The two of us met once a week, and she guided me through each step. Immediately, my life started to improve. The steps were helping me to be able to surrender everything to God and to put Him first in my life. Going to meetings every day gave me the support and encouragement I needed to feel hope and a new sense of purpose in my life.

My newfound freedom from alcohol, however, only seemed to be making my marriage struggles worse. At first, my husband did not want to stop drinking or hanging out with our drinking buddies, which made it hard for me to remain sober. After a few months, we started going to counseling, and he agreed to stop drinking and seeing his friends. After that, it felt like old times, when things were good between us. I started to believe that everything was going to work out with our marriage.

Then one afternoon, he told me that he had plans to go drinking with the guys. I was devastated. How could he choose alcohol over me and our marriage? I resented him for that, and for the fact that he could drink and I could not.

Alone in the house, the resentment turned to anger. I wanted to lash out. At that moment, I decided to go buy some alcohol and get drunk. When he came home, he would see what he had done to me.

Each month that you stay sober, my twelve-step group would give out poker chips as a reward. I had been keeping all of mine in my car, so if I felt the desire to drink, the sight of the chips and the reminder of how far I'd come would help me to keep going.

I went out to my vehicle, took all my chips, and threw them all over the kitchen floor. *There, that will show him.*

I had eleven chips. I was only two weeks away from a full year of sobriety. But in my state of rage and desperation, I was sure that the only way to save my marriage was to show my husband how important it was for him to change his lifestyle, too. He had to understand how much his actions had hurt me.

I grabbed my purse, headed out the door, and jumped in my car. My head was spinning as I started driving to the store to purchase alcohol. One voice was telling me that I couldn't throw away almost a year of hard work. My relationship with God had become stronger than it has ever been, and I had all my new friends who loved and supported me. I had finally been able to start loving myself and was finding out who I was. I had new purpose, and God was healing me and helping me to help others. But the other voice was telling me that the only way to save my marriage was to begin drinking again. I had been married almost 40 years—what would I do without my husband? How would a divorce affect our children?

As I drove, I realized that I wasn't going to the store. Some impulse, unknown to me at the time, had taken over my hands and had me driving to the recovery center where my meetings were held.

It was mid-afternoon, and there weren't any meetings at the center at that time. No one would even be at the building. Even so, I found myself pulling into the parking lot. I looked over at a picnic table, and there sat my sponsor. I couldn't believe it.

I sat down at the table across from her. "I didn't expect to see you here today."

"I was supposed to meet someone, but they never came." She must have seen that I was struggling, because she reached out and took my hands. I immediately felt the love flowing into me. She listened as I shared and told her that I wanted to drink, that I was sure that was the answer. She prayed for me and begged me not to drink. She reminded me how special I am, and how much God loves me.

Then she looked at me and asked, "Is God on vacation?"

"No," I answered.

"Do you trust Him?"

"Yes, of course I do."

She shook her head. "No, you don't."

I realized in that moment she was right. If I truly trusted God, I would let Him be in control. My sponsor had been

> But since we belong to the day, let us be sober, putting on faith and love as a breastplate, and the hope of salvation as a helmet.
>
> —1 THESSALONIANS 5:8 (NIV)

telling me all year that she would love me until I could love myself, and that I should look at myself in the mirror every day and say, "I love you." I felt her love then and there, felt God's love through her, and realized that while I loved my husband, I was starting to love myself more.

Suddenly, the urge to drink was lifted! God's love had driven it out! God had used this earthly angel to set me free.

Two weeks later, on the Fourth of July, my sponsor handed me my one-year medallion. My divorce was final the following year. I became more involved in the program and started helping others. I also got involved in a local church and went on a mission trip. I met a wonderful man in the program, and we have been married almost 5 years. We are retired and travel all over the country bringing hope to those still suffering. For the first time in my life, at 65 years old, I have found healing and peace!

> For this God is our God for ever and ever; he will be our guide even to the end.
>
> —PSALM 48:14 (NIV)

I had once thought I knew what my future would look like and couldn't imagine it any other way. When I finally let God take control, He gave me the peace of knowing that everything is going to be OK if I trust in Him. God had led both my sponsor and me to that parking lot that afternoon to protect me from a relapse.

As I write this, I'm just two weeks away from receiving my medallion for 9 years of sobriety. The desire to drink has never returned. God loves me and is always with me. He wants the absolute best for me. All I must do is give it all over to Him and trust Him.

...But God
Kelly Farley

It was April 7, 2012, the Saturday before Easter. The weather was perfect, and we had several fun activities planned. My daughter had to work that morning, so I took my son, Justin, to church for an Easter egg hunt and youth activities. In the afternoon, my husband met us at my in-laws for our annual family egg hunt. It was such a fun day. No one was prepared for the tragic turn this day would take.

The adults hid the eggs at my in-laws' house, but this year, we only had two kids collecting them: Justin, who was 13, and his younger cousin, Spencer. Justin collected all the eggs he wanted and decided to climb the large maple tree in his grandparents' yard, a tree he had climbed all his life. His dad—my husband, Bill—had just permitted him to climb higher, and the rest of us were busy talking and helping Spencer find the remaining eggs.

I walked away from Justin, leaving him to climb the tree, and headed toward the backyard. Then I heard a sound I will never forget—the sound of a tree limb snapping. I turned to see Justin falling. In my mind, it was as if it happened in slow motion. I even had time to wonder, *How is he falling head first?* I yelled his name, hoping he would rotate or flip himself somehow. *This isn't happening,* I insisted to myself. But it was. My son landed on his neck and left shoulder and lay motionless on the ground at the base of the tree.

I ran to him. "Are you OK?"

He didn't answer verbally; he could only flail his arms, a bit uncontrolled, and that was it. I knew he wasn't OK, but, in denial, I told my husband to check on him and tell me when to call 911.

I walked away, dropped to my knees, and prayed, crying out to God, "Please help my son." I knew I couldn't do anything to help Justin, so I turned to the only One who could.

My prayer was interrupted by Bill telling me to call 911. My mind was racing, and I had difficulty putting my thoughts together; even dialing 911 took effort. After making that call, I called my pastor and asked him to pray.

The ambulance arrived and the paramedics told us they were taking Justin to Big Wake, a distant trauma center. Of all the hospitals, why that one? Bill rode in the ambulance with Justin, and my father-in-law drove me. On the way, I called my daughter to tell her about her brother and where we were heading.

The ambulance took Justin to the trauma center in the adult ER. Bill followed Justin into the trauma room and locked eyes with a familiar face. One of the trauma nurses happened to be an old employee of our family business. Her shift was over, but she stayed with Bill and Justin. Her presence gave Bill some comfort as they worked on Justin.

It was surreal walking into the trauma center and asking to see my son. I couldn't figure out why my child was at the adult ER instead of the children's. Shortly after finding Bill and getting a quick update, I saw Justin lying on the table with all these doctors and nurses working on him.

The next thing I knew, a doctor called us into the hall. She was the head of the trauma department. She pulled up his X-rays and told us that Justin had broken his neck and had an incomplete spinal cord injury with paralysis. Then she said the words no parent wants to hear: "I am sorry, but there is nothing else we can do."

My heart sank; I looked at Bill, thinking. *What are we going to do now?* We were in shock and disbelief.

As we turned around, the head of pediatrics approached us. He told us he was walking through the ER to check on another patient and heard about our son. He said he wanted to transfer him to the pediatric ICU and put him in a medically induced hypothermic coma for three days. The treatment had been used successfully for older patients who suffered brain injuries, but they had never done the procedure on a pediatric patient with a spinal cord injury before. It could potentially help Justin and reduce the swelling within his spinal cord. The doctor said, "If it were my son, this is what I would do."

> "... but God intended it for good to accomplish what is now being done, the saving of many lives. So then, don't be afraid."
>
> —GENESIS 50:20–21 (NIV)

After the trauma doctor told us there was nothing else they could do to help with Justin's paralysis, there was at least a shred of hope. Yes! Of course, we wanted to do that. But first, we had to meet with the on-call neurosurgeon to make sure that the surgery to stabilize the broken bones in his neck could be delayed.

Walking into the private waiting room, I was overwhelmed—it was full of friends and family, who just wanted to be there to show love, support us, and offer prayers. Then the neurosurgeon came in and told us his qualifications; even though he had never operated on a child before, he was confident he could do the operation on our son. Before he would approve delaying the surgery, we needed an MRI to confirm that Justin did not have damage that needed immediate attention. Once the MRI was completed, the neurosurgeon approved waiting, so we agreed to proceed with the hypothermic coma treatment.

We returned to the room where Justin was waiting. I had a chance to ask Justin if he knew what had happened. He told me he reached up to grab the higher branch and had to jump up to reach it; that branch broke, and the branch he had been standing on caught his feet, flipping him upside down. I then told him the doctor wanted to put him in a coma. He asked what that was, and we told him they would put him to sleep for three days; he seemed relieved and said he would like to sleep. The team prepared to induce the coma, and the pediatric doctor came in, introduced himself to Justin, and asked if he had any nicknames.

"My nickname is Bob."

"That's pretty unusual," the doctor said. "Why Bob?"

"That's what my youth pastor calls me."

Upon hearing this, the doctor asked if he could pray with us before he induced the coma. This prayer was a confirmation that God had heard my prayers and that everything would be OK.

As they prepared to induce a coma in Justin, the nurse told us to go to the pediatric ICU; when the procedure was complete, they would bring Justin up to his room, and we could see him. We went to the PICU waiting area and decided one of us would be with Justin at all times, while the other needed to be home with our 16-year-old daughter, Logan. As hard as it was to leave Justin, we knew we had to be well-rested to be the best we could be for him, Logan, and each other. I went home that night, and Bill stayed with Justin.

I didn't know what to expect when I walked into Justin's room the next day. All the monitors, wires, and fluids pumping into him were so strange. I will never forget the despair on my husband's face as he stood beside Justin's bed, just watching him lying there. At this moment, Bill blamed himself. "What kind of future will he have?"

"We can't be hopeless," I told him. "We must be hopeful. With Jesus, we have hope. He is our hope!" I had a peace about me that I couldn't explain, one that reminded me of the peace that surpasses all understanding as Paul described in his letter to the Philippians.

> **And the peace of God, which transcends all understanding, will guard your hearts and your minds in Christ Jesus.**
>
> —PHILIPPIANS 4:7 (NIV)

The neurosurgeon came to show us the MRI scans. Justin had fractured his C3 and C6 vertebrae and crushed the C4 and C5. The neurosurgeon confirmed that he was confident he could do the surgery, but wanted to ensure we were good with him being the one to do it. Afterward, he told me that the pediatric neurosurgeon on call the night of Justin's accident was a brain specialist, and here he was, a spine specialist. Wow, God!

They cooled Justin's body to 93 degrees for 48 hours. During this time, Justin sometimes awoke, dazed, and the nurses would check his pupils and extremities and calmly talk him back to sleep. They assured us he wouldn't remember anything. At 10:53 Monday night, they started to warm him up slowly. Surgery was scheduled for 4 p.m. Wednesday.

Surgery was a success, and Justin woke up with a newfound sense of humor. I think this was a blessing from God. Justin always seemed to have a smile on his face, and he made comments and jokes that kept his nurses laughing.

Physical therapy started right away. On the initial assessment, Justin had no movement on his left side and limited movement on his right. Despite my doubts, my husband kept telling Justin, a roller hockey player, that he would skate again, even though this is not what the doctors said. They didn't expect Justin to walk again.

> **We are hard pressed on every side, but not crushed; perplexed, but not in despair; persecuted, but not abandoned; struck down, but not destroyed.**
>
> —2 CORINTHIANS 4:8–9 (NIV)

My friend Kim started a Facebook event as one central place where we could update everyone and so people could pray. Soon, that page had over 4,500 people following Justin's

recovery. I was the one who kept the page updated. Each day had its struggles, but I was determined to focus on the positive and how God was showing up with each day's miracle. I didn't know what God would do, but I knew too many people were watching for Him not to do something miraculous.

Justin would spend a total of 3 weeks in the PICU before being sent to Levine's Children's Hospital for 6 weeks of inpatient physical therapy. Every day, they had to rethink his treatment plan because he was already past that day's skill. We promised Justin that he would walk out of that hospital, and on June 7, he did! He continued physical therapy throughout the summer, and in August, he started high school. As he headed to the car for the first day of school, he didn't take his wheelchair!

Justin is now happily married and started his own towing company in 2019. While not 100 percent healed yet, he can do whatever he wants. He is walking and active, and yes, he has even put on his hockey skates and skated again. If you were to meet him today, you would never know that something so tragic had happened to him.

That Easter weekend was tragic and life-changing. Justin should have died when he fell from that tree, or in the best case been paralyzed for life. But God had different plans. Instead of a funeral, He saved my son's life. Instead of fear and paralysis, He directed the steps of paramedics, nurses, and doctors. Instead of isolation and uncertainty, His church was His hands and feet, with prayers, meals, hugs, financial gifts, and acts of service during our greatest time of need.

My life as a casual Christian was over; after experiencing the Lord in such a visible, personal way, I wanted to know Him more.

In the Crosshairs
Diana DeSpain Schramer

As Dad and I pulled up to Mom's ranch home to pick up my 4-year-old brother, Stevie, for the weekend, we saw Mom standing in the window, watching for us, her face etched with misery. Mom and Dad had divorced two years earlier when I was 11. Dad had received custody of me, and Mom of Stevie.

"Well, this doesn't look good," Dad said to me as he turned into the driveway. "I wonder what's going on now."

I jumped out of the car and ran up to the house while Dad waited in the car. Mom opened the door before I had a chance to knock, her face pale and tight and her body crackling with tension. I took a tentative step inside and cast a wary glance around the kitchen, my instincts on red alert.

The second Stevie saw me he burst into tears and ran to me from the living room. "Boy got really mad at Mom, and he threw a glass at her, and it hit the wall, and it broke!" he blurted, growing more agitated with every word while barely taking a breath. Stevie was by nature a laid-back, happy-go-lucky little guy who viewed everything as a grand adventure. But not now. "Let's go, Diana! Let's go!" he cried, frantic, as he pulled me toward the door.

I looked into the living room from where I was standing. Mom's boyfriend, who Stevie called Boy, was leaning forward on the couch in the center of the room, his forearms resting on his knees with a burning cigarette clenched between his thick fingers. His unblinking black eyes glared at the TV on the opposite side of the room. An open bottle of whiskey and an array of beer cans littered the coffee table in front of him, along with an overflowing ashtray. Mom had retreated to the far corner of the living room behind the couch, standing with her arms wrapped tight around her waist and her large, round, chocolate-brown eyes wide and watchful with fear.

I have to get us out of here, I thought to myself. I looked down at the floor and saw Stevie's packed bag by the door.

Suddenly, shouting erupted between Mom and Boy, the ensuing chaos rendering their words incomprehensible. As their argument and the hostility between them escalated, Boy jumped up from the couch and stormed into the bedroom. Mom bolted across the living room to Stevie and me, picked up his bag, pushed it into my arms, and shoved us toward the door. "He's getting his gun! He's getting his gun!" she whisper-yelled at us, her eyes flooded with terror.

> **The LORD will fight for you; you need only to be still.**
>
> —EXODUS 14:14 (NIV)

Stevie ripped open the door and fled outside to Dad's car, his unzipped parka flapping around him like the wings of a bat. I was right behind him, clutching his bag, leaping through the mounds of snow.

Dad's black eyes were round as moons when Stevie and I landed inside the car, both of us hysterical, crying and screaming, "He's getting his gun! He's getting his gun!"

"What?!" Dad said.

"He's getting his gun!" Steve and I shouted in unison.

"Boy and Mom have been fighting all day! He threw a glass at Mom, and it hit the wall, and it broke!" Stevie cried, wiping the snot running down to his lip with his sleeve.

Dad opened his car door.

My heart stopped. "Dad! Where are you going??"

"You two stay here," he said, calm yet steely. "I'll be right back."

"Dad, don't go! He's got a gun!" My now-hammering heart threatened to explode in my chest. Desperate to stop Dad from walking up to that house, I pleaded, "Dad, don't go! He will shoot you, Dad!" Stevie and I were crying harder now.

"He's not going to shoot me. I'll be right back. But you two stay here." Dad arched his thick black eyebrows and gave me his "and I mean it" look, knowing full well that I would run after him, trying to stop him. But he also knew that Stevie would be right behind me, and that I would never endanger him. Dad was right on both counts.

Dad got out of the car, slamming the door behind him. Stevie, from the center of the back seat, and I, from the passenger seat in the front, watched helplessly as Dad marched through the snow up to the house on a mission.

I was terrified that in a matter of minutes Stevie and I could not only witness both of our parents being shot to death, but we could also be orphaned. If Boy didn't then kill us too, that is. *Please, please, Jesus, please protect us*, I prayed in my heart. My body was frozen like a statue while the blood thundered in my ears.

"Are we gonna be OK, Diana?" Stevie said, his voice shaking.

When I turned around and met his tear-filled hazel eyes wide with fear, my maternal instincts kicked in.

"Yes, Stevie. We're going to be OK." *I just don't know how. Jesus, please help!* I could barely breathe from panic, but held myself in check so as not to upset Stevie now that he was calming down. Dark scenarios ran through my mind as I started to plan what I would do if Mom and Dad were shot, if I had to drive Stevie and myself to safety. Yet despite the terror pumping throughout my body, deep in my spirit I felt a glimmer of peace, instinctively knowing that, if I needed to, Jesus would show me how to drive Dad's car and that He would deliver Stevie and me to safety.

The door to the house opened and Boy stuck his head out. I held my breath, bracing for the crack of gunfire and the horror of seeing Dad shot point-blank.

Dad started talking. And talking. His body appeared relaxed, but Dad always grew eerily still when he was most angry. Like a coiled cobra ready to strike, his eyes were riveted on Boy's head suspended in the doorway, which bobbled perpetually as if he were saying, "Yes, sir. Yes, sir. Yes, sir."

> "For we have no power to face this vast army that is attacking us. We do not know what to do, but our eyes are on you."
>
> —2 CHRONICLES 20:12 (NIV)

Mom appeared in the doorway next to Boy. Dad said something to her, and she responded. Dad hesitated a moment, his eyes now fixed on Mom. After a couple of seconds, he said something else to her, to which she responded. Dad then turned on his heel, stepped down from the porch, and walked back toward Stevie and me in the car. I held my breath and

Wrapped *in* His Protection | 233

gripped the door handle with a vise grip, waiting for a hail of bullets to erupt from the house.

Dad climbed into the car and turned the key in the ignition, strangely calm considering the fact that none of us was yet in the clear. Mom and Boy disappeared behind their closing front door.

When I could finally speak, I said, "I was so scared he was going to shoot you, Dad." I sucked in my breath, trying to slow my heart that was still hammering like kettledrums. Unlike Dad and Stevie, I did not—and still don't—calm down quickly. It would be days before I recovered from this incident.

> "This is what the LORD says to you: 'Do not be afraid or discouraged because of this vast army. For the battle is not yours, but God's.'"
>
> —2 CHRONICLES 20:15 (NIV)

"He wasn't going to shoot me. He's not going to shoot anybody," Dad said with certainty as he pulled out of the driveway onto the rural Illinois state highway. "And I told him that he had better *never* threaten one of my kids *again*!"

Stevie and I exchanged a wide-eyed, sidelong glance.

"I also told him that I had better not see one mark on your mother either."

I turned to look at the house as we drove away. As when we had pulled up, Mom stood in the front window, looking back at me, her dark eyes in her white, drawn face etched with even deeper misery.

"Dad, wait!" I grabbed his arm. "Mom's standing in the window! We have to go back!"

Dad shook his head. "I told her to pack her things and come with us, but she said no."

"But we can't leave her here! We have to go back!"

Dad shook his head again. "I told her we would wait, but she said no. She wanted to stay." He looked at me and shrugged, baffled. "Honey, she made her choice. There's nothing more I can do." As confusing as it was, I knew that was true. Dad could not force Mom to leave with us. She had made clear her decision to stay, which was hers to make.

Mom's and Boy's volatile on-again, off-again relationship continued for another decade. However, the threat to Stevie and me that day was an isolated incident. As he had before, Boy treated us both with genuine warmth and kindness. And his affection for Stevie was palpable and sincere. Still, a turbulent relationship and alcohol abuse are chaotic companions at best and deadly at worst.

That scenario could have taken a tragic turn. But instead, by God's incomprehensible power, Dad's confrontation defused the situation. Only God could have done that.

Fifty years later, I still shudder when I think about what could have happened that day. And I still am in awe of God's protection and deliverance, not only of Stevie and myself, but also of Dad, Mom, and Boy.

Healing Hands
Kathlyn C. White

God is with us. God is in us. God is around us. God is working through us. If we believe and do not doubt, God will do amazing things in our lives. He still heals today. Sometimes it is astounding. Sometimes it is perplexing. And, in my case, it was very unexpected.

It was the early 1990s, and I had only been a Christian for a few years. Despite growing up in the church, I wrestled with doubts about God. But once I overcame these doubts, my faith was strong. I was reading my Bible. I believed in miracles. I believed in healings. I believed if God made us and the world around us, he could heal whatever was wrong with us.

I couldn't get enough of God once I had prayed to receive Jesus Christ as my personal savior. I watched a lot of television shows about God and how he heals today. Healing had taken on a new significance for me because after years of mysterious uterine bleeding, I had finally been properly diagnosed with a uterine fibroid. By the time they discovered it, it was the size of a grapefruit. Removing a mass that large could have serious complications, and the doctor had me donate my own blood just in case I lost too much during the surgery. The surgery was scheduled for February, so there was nothing left to do but wait, pray, and trust God.

One of my favorite Bible teaching shows was led by television evangelist Marilyn Hickey. She taught the Bible and told stories of how she had laid hands on many people and healed them of their ailments. She revealed as she preached that she had a special gift for healing growths such as warts, tumors, etc. She was a strong, godly woman, and I greatly enjoyed learning from her.

One September morning as I was watching Marilyn Hickey on television, I felt a presence in my room. The energy in the room was palpable, and I knew it was God. I felt in awe and a little afraid of this unseen presence.

At that moment in the broadcast, Marilyn invited her viewers to go to Russia with her on a mission trip a few months later, in January. I've never wanted to go to Russia, and I hated flying, so this was not an appealing idea to me. I was working at the time and also had two small children and a husband at home. It is not a choice I would have made on my own, but when God showed up in my bedroom, I understood I was receiving a strong calling to go on this mission trip. At first, I told the Lord I did not want to go. His presence intensified, and I realized that I could not argue with the Lord if this was His will. If God wanted me to go, I had to go, so I humbly said, "Yes, Lord."

> **I will take away sickness from among you.**
>
> —EXODUS 23:25 (NIV)

When I told my husband what had happened, he was totally supportive of my feelings, my impression from God, and my faith that God had called me. He told me to go, and we both believed God would take care of the details.

I signed up for the mission trip shortly after the Lord came to me in my bedroom. There was no reason to hesitate. I didn't want to let the Lord down.

The day of departure finally came and I flew to Atlanta where I boarded a plane for Russia. Marilyn had arranged for her mission trip to take place in various cities along the Volga River; we would travel by boat, allowing us to access some of Russia's major cities as well as small towns along the river. We attended classes in the evening while we were on the boat, and during the day small groups of volunteers went into the impoverished towns along the river. We handed out tracts written in Russian and presented the Gospel with the help of translators.

> **But when you ask, you must believe and not doubt.**
>
> —JAMES 1:6 (NIV)

The last night of the trip, Marilyn scheduled a service at which she would preach and lay hands on anyone who came and requested it. On the day of the service, we all gathered together in an old, dirty, run-down auditorium and waited for the countrymen and women to gather and be healed.

The word about this healing service spread quickly around the city, and masses of people attended. Russia was full of people needing a touch from the Lord. The people poured into the auditorium, and after Marilyn had preached, she called for anyone in the audience to come forward for her to lay hands on them.

That night, Marilyn Hickey laid hands on my abdomen. When she touched me, I felt an energy surge through my body, and I took a step back. I knew something had happened. When I got back to the room, I noticed that my pants were looser. I slept well that evening. The next morning, we readied ourselves for the flight back home.

Back home, I made an appointment with my doctor in preparation for a partial hysterectomy. I was very nervous. I even asked the doctor if a friend of mine who was a nurse could be in the operating room to observe and support me. The wonderful doctor agreed. It did not occur to me to ask for another ultrasound to see if the fibroid was still there. While I had faith, I did not yet have the spiritual maturity to consider that God might have healed me in a way that would have made the surgery unnecessary.

On the day of the surgery, I nervously asked the doctor if he would pray for me. He did and I drifted under, thanks to the anesthesia. The surgery was expected to be long and drawn out due to the size of the fibroid. But when the doctor cut me open, all he found was a small, shriveled-up remnant of a fibroid. He was in shock. His tests had shown a much larger growth, and he had been prepared for the worst.

My husband was in the waiting room during the surgery. He later told me that the doctor had estimated the surgery would be about one hour. When the doctor came out to the waiting room after only 20 minutes, my husband feared the worst. However, the doctor had only good news: because the fibroid was so much smaller than they had expected, the surgery was done quickly and without the dangers associated with removing a larger mass. My husband immediately realized our prayers had been answered.

> "Everything is possible for him who believes."
>
> —MARK 9:23 (NIV)

When I woke up and heard what the doctor had found, I was amazed by the miracle that had occurred. There was no way to explain what had occurred medically. The doctor was a Christian, but I don't think he had ever witnessed anything like this. There was no doubt a touch from God had shrunk

GOD'S GIFT OF SIGHT
— Linda L. Kruschke —

IN JOHN 9, Jesus gave a man the ultimate gift: sight. What many take for granted, this man had never experienced because he was born blind. This miraculous healing was bestowed in a mundane way. Jesus "spit on the ground, made some mud with the saliva, and put it on the man's eyes. 'Go,' he told him, 'wash in the Pool of Siloam'" (John 9:6–7, NIV). Rather than thinking the solution too easy, the man did as Jesus commanded and received the gift of sight for his obedience and faith. This story teaches us that God longs to open the spiritual eyes of those who obey in faith.

---

the fibroid. God had healed me in a profound way. And what a witness for the doctor and medical staff!

I went on to a full recovery and an even deeper faith. What an amazing God we serve. He wants to heal us, if we just believe. God healed me and protected me from a potentially life-threatening surgical outcome. While the doctor planned for the worst, God planned for my best possible outcome. God is an active God, doing more for us than we could hope for. We just need to have faith and open our hearts to His work.

Contributors

Sandra Ardoin   p. 89
Robin Ayscue   p. 31
Mindy Baker   pp. 110, 195
Jeannie Blackmer   p. 1
Rebecca D. Bruner   p. 158
Heidi Chiavaroli   pp. 18, 171
Elsa Kok Colopy   p. 59
Kerry Duprez   p. 212
Elizabeth Erlandson   p. 145
Kelly Farley   p. 223
Joe Fletcher   p. 26
Kelsey Green   p. 152
Lynne Hartke   p. 76
Kim Taylor Henry   pp. 38, 113
Robin T. Jennings   p. 78
Linda L. Kruschke   pp. 164, 176, 197, 240
Barbara Latta   p. 199
Shannon Leach   p. 46
Stacy Leicht   p. 140
Jennifer Andrus Lindstrom   p. 12
Cynthia A. Lovely   p. 121
Eryn Lynum   pp. 16, 132
Linda Marie   p. 35

Claire McGarry   p. 212
Roberta Messner   p. 54
Christel Owoo   p. 83
Kristen Paris   p. 22
Amanda Pennock   p. 219
John Peterson   p. 40
Elizabeth Renicks   p. 62
Betty A. Rodgers-Kulich   p. 104
Diana DeSpain Schramer   p. 230
Kimberly Shumate   p. 53
Ingrid Skarstad   p. 206
Wendy Lynne Smith   pp. 40, 133
Jeanne Takenaka   p. 177
Lori Tanabe   p. 183
Cecil Taylor   p. 166
Terrie Todd   p. 218
Mary Vee   p. 69
Tina Wanamaker   p. 95
Carolyn Waverly   pp. 115, 189
Kathlyn C. White   p. 236
Stephanie A. Wilsey   p. 126

Acknowledgments

Every attempt has been made to credit the sources of copyrighted material used in this book. If any such acknowledgment has been inadvertently omitted or miscredited, receipt of such information would be appreciated.

Scripture quotations marked (AMPC) are taken from the *Amplified Bible, Classic Edition*. Copyright © 1954, 1958, 1962, 1964, 1965, 1987 by The Lockman Foundation.

Scripture quotations marked (ESV) are taken from *The Holy Bible, English Standard Version*. Copyright © 2001 by Crossway Bibles, a division of Good News Publishers. Used by permission. All rights reserved.

Scripture quotations marked (NIV) are taken from *The Holy Bible, New International Version*®, *NIV*®. Copyright © 1973, 1978, 1984, 2011 by Biblica, Inc. Used by permission. All rights reserved worldwide.

Scripture quotations marked (NKJV) are taken from the *New King James Version*®. Copyright © 1982 by Thomas Nelson. Used by permission. All rights reserved.

Scripture quotations marked (NLT) are taken from the *Holy Bible, New Living Translation*. Copyright © 1996, 2004, 2007, 2015 by Tyndale House Foundation. Used by permission of Tyndale House Publishers Inc., Carol Stream, Illinois. All rights reserved.

A Note from the Editors

We hope you enjoyed *Wrapped in His Protection*, published by Guideposts. For more than 75 years, Guideposts, a nonprofit organization, has been driven by a vision of a world filled with hope. We aspire to be the voice of a trusted friend, a friend who makes you feel more hopeful and connected.

By making a purchase from Guideposts, you join our community in touching millions of lives, inspiring them to believe that all things are possible through faith, hope, and prayer. Your continued support allows us to provide uplifting resources to those in need. Whether through our communities, websites, apps, or publications, we inspire our audiences, bring them together, and comfort, uplift, entertain, and guide them. Visit us at guideposts.org to learn more.

We would love to hear from you. Write us at Guideposts, P.O. Box 5815, Harlan, Iowa 51593 or call us at (800) 932-2145. Did you love *Wrapped in His Protection*? Leave a review for this product on guideposts.org/shop. Your feedback helps others in our community find relevant products.

Find inspiration, find faith, find Guideposts.
Shop our best sellers and favorites at
guideposts.org/shop
Or scan the QR code to go directly to our Shop

Printed in the United States
by Baker & Taylor Publisher Services